ISLE OF THE UNKNOWN

AUTHOR
GEOFFREY MCKINNEY

ARTISTS
AMOS ORION STERNS
JASON RAINVILLE
CYNTHIA SHEPPARD

EDITOR
JAMES EDWARD RAGGI IV

Isle of the Unknown
© Geoffrey McKinney 2011
First Edition, First Printing 2011
Published by Lamentations of the Flame Princess
Cover llustration by Cynthia Sheppard
Monster Illustrations by Amos Orion Sterns
Magic-User Illustrations and Cartography by Jason Rainville
Layout by Mattias Wikström/TIGERBYTE
Isle of the Unknown Logo by Matt Johnsen
Printed in Finland by Otava Book Printing Ltd
ISBN 978-952-5904-25-3

CONTENTS

Introduction for the Referee 4
Legends 6
Hex Descriptions 8
Monsters 116
Magical Statues 121
Magic-Users 124
Clerics 125
Towns 125
Cities 125

INTRODUCTION
FOR THE REFEREE

THIS BOOK describes an island nearly 35,000 square miles in size. Using traditional fantasy role-playing rules, the Referee can conduct adventures upon the Isle of the Unknown. It can be placed anywhere in the Referee's campaign world, or it can serve as the basis of a new campaign, or as the setting for one-shot adventures.

One point of interest is described for each of the map's 330 land hexes. None of the monsters, magic spells, magic items, etc. in this book has been taken from any previously published role-playing game product. This will help ensure freshness and a sense of wonder and newness as your players explore a realm that is truly unknown.

Since each hex covers over 86 square miles of territory, much more can be found in a hex than the supplied point of interest. The author assumes that most encounters will be with men or with mundane animals, but other Referees might decide otherwise. The wise Referee will use or ignore the hex descriptions as he sees fit. He need never be caught unprepared. Regardless which hex players wander into, the Referee will always have something at hand.

To aid the Referee, only the weird, fantastical, and magical is described herein. The mundane is left to the discretion of the campaign Referee, to be supplied according to the characteristics of his own conceptions or campaign world. Detailed encounter tables of (for example) French knights, monks, pilgrims, etc. would be of scant use to a Referee whose campaign

world is a fantasy version of pre-Columbian America. Similar considerations led to the exclusion of most proper names. In preparing this book, the author assumed the following:

The societies, flora, and fauna of this predominantly mountainous and wooded isle resemble those of the French territory of Auvergne circa A.D. 1311. The island's highest elevation reaches 8,900 feet, and the most common trees are various types of pines as well as aspens. The human population numbers approximately 70,000. Though only places with a population of at least 1,500 are noted in the hex descriptions, many hamlets, villages, thorps, etc. dot the island. Ruins (similar to Roman ruins of circa A.D. 200) of a previous civilization are found throughout the island.

Of course, the Referee might wish to consider the island as Polynesian, or African, or Asian, or Atlantean, or Lemurian, or something else entirely. In any and all cases, the pontifical Referee is encouraged to change things to suit his whims.

LEGENDS

THE REFEREE might wish to give the player characters knowledge of legends regarding the Isle of the Unknown before they begin exploring. Perhaps each player character will know 1–3 legends (or more or fewer, according to the dictates of the Referee). Following are thirty sample legends. The first 19 are truthful (as far as they go), and the hex number to which each refers is given. The relative truthfulness or falsity of the last 11 legends is for the Referee to determine.

1. He who pricks his finger upon the trident of the sea king will become lord of sea creatures. *(Hex 0503)*
2. Touch the yellow songbird statue to understand birdsong. *(Hex 0805)*
3. Speak the magic word to gain the red scale armor. *(Hex 0816)*
4. Beware the bewitching statue clad only in her honey-gold hair! *(Hex 0902)*
5. Blossoms given to the flower-maiden will make a healing draught. *(Hex 0909)*
6. Receive the blessing of the naked woman to be healed of all hurts. *(Hex 0911)*
7. For victory over those that fly, bloody your hand upon the lance of him seated upon the winged mount. *(Hex 1010)*
8. Whisper to Mercury your message, and it will be delivered. *(Hex 1102)*
9. Ask her of icy blue to point your way. (Hex 1110)

10 Add your sword to the pile to avoid death. *(Hex 1402)*
11 Touch your weapons to the unclothed woman's knife to satisfy your vengeance. *(Hex 1411)*
12 Crush the purple stone set in the golden ring to banish the bear of black and white. *(Hex 1810)*
13 The golden fleece heals, but thieves beware! *(Hex 1907)*
14 The Amazon deals death to those with no womb. *(Hex 1909)*
15 Those garbed in red from head to toe can approach the great pillar of fire unscorched. *(Hex 2009)*
16 Magic-users touching the statue of a graybeard will obtain weal or woe. *(Hex 2010)*
17 Touch the Medusa to gain the power of her mythical gaze. *(Hex 2311)*
18 The moon-maiden will grant a magical gift to those who give her the moon's metal. *(Hex 2313)*
19 Shun the isle warded by the sea king. *(Hex 2316)*
20 The Isle of the Unknown is the last remnant of foundered Atlantis.
21 The ancient men of the Isle of the Unknown formed thirteen kingdoms.
22 Millennia ago upon the Isle of the Unknown lived a mighty mage who fashioned uncounted magical statues.
23 Deep in the forest an evil, sentient flower rules an empire of plants served by human slaves.
24 The first men of the Isle of the Unknown had skin hues unlike those of men today.
25 The elderly bishop's closest friend, a pious young archpriest, is a secret diabolist with designs to become the next bishop.
26 In a hidden underground realm rules the Yellow King, who commands that everything in his domain be colored yellow.
27 Diabolists have made an unholy pact with the giant sea worms that squirm in the depths.
28 In the Palace of Tiles, press first the blue, then the red, and finally the green tile to find wondrous treasures.
29 Upon the island is a gateway between worlds.
30 Buried treasure and secret pirate havens dot the coasts of the island.

HEX
DESCRIPTIONS

0115

0114 In a humble cottage of unhewn stone lives a pious 4th-level cleric (ARMOR: plate + shield, HD 4, HP 12, MOVE 60') who keeps but does not wear a red surcoat with a white cross. His broad sword and mace hang in easy reach upon the wall. Seven years ago, the cleric first experienced the miracle of bi-location. While still in his dwelling, he found himself also in the Land of Water and Copper far over the Western Ocean. The people of this land were beardless and had straight black hair and red skin. Though nearly naked, these people were crowned with gaudily bright feathers of great length and intricacy. Most fabulous of all, even their lowliest ranks wore golden jewelry. In this far land, gold is so common that it is used as a mere decoration. Even small children, naked save for their golden jewelry, walk wheresoever they will unafraid and unmolested. The stone cities of these people stand amidst jungles beneath the shadows of vast, stepped pyramids. The cleric will show to trusted visitors a curiously-carved golden torc (worth 200 g.p.) given to him by this exotic people. If the cleric is slain, he has a 15% chance of still being alive because he was in two places at the time of his "death."

0115 A 300 lb. skunk (ARMOR: as leather + shield, HD 9, HP 43, MOVE 150', 1d10/bite, 1d6/projectile) has a body as thin and sinuous as a snake, and its head is crowned with deer horns. It can shoot an essentially unlimited number of its claws with the same range as a long bow.

0116   The sparklingly-clear blue waters on all but the eastern shore of the island reveal submerged white marble ruins of the Classic Period of ancient Greece. If a diver manages to approach the graceful structures, they will waver and vanish before his eyes. After he surfaces, the ruins will be visible to him once again.

0214   A 30' tall statue of an iron Titan holds aloft a javelin. It is surrounded by a 60' radius circle of lifeless land. Anyone daring to step in the circle will cause the statue to animate (ARMOR: as plate + shield, HD 14, HP 63, MOVE 40', 4d12/javelin) and attack. If its intended victims try to flee, the statue will cause the earth to tremble by stamping its sandaled feet upon the ground. All within 200' must save or fall to the ground, unable to act until the next round.

0215   By a small lake stands the manse of the Mage of Mirrors, an old 6th-level magic-user (ARMOR: none, HD 6, HP 16, MOVE 90'). Mirrors almost completely cover the walls and ceiling. The Mirror Mage's presence within the house makes its multitude of ordinary mirrors magical. Typically, gazing into the mirrors brings one visions of the distant past (with saurian behemoths crashing through luxuriant jungle) or of the distant future (full of surfaces of shiny metals and glittering lights). A person within the house, however, will begin to feel that inside the mirrors is the actual world and that he inhabits an insubstantial reflection. If he fails a saving throw, he will unknowingly begin to take 1d6 points of damage per round as he stares intently into a mirror. When his hit points fall to 0, he will fade into the mirror like a morning mist before the sun.

Regarding Magical Statues: Unless otherwise noted, these ancient statues are so luxurious that they verge upon the barbaric, in the style of the Latin decadence of the final centuries of the Western Roman Empire. Any weapons or other items possessed by magical statues have no special qualities when used by anyone other than the statue. They are immune to weathering.

ISLE OF THE UNKNOWN

0216 By a small creek grows a fairy ring (5' diameter) in vividly green grass. The mushrooms have purple caps with yellow stems and warts. Gravity does not exist inside the fairy ring. Anyone or anything placed inside it will float 3' off the ground.

0307

0307 A 180 lb. weasel (ARMOR: none, HD 5, HP 29, MOVE 150' [walk], 50' [tunnel], 1d6+1/claw) can tunnel even through solid stone. It appears to have four large-fanged vipers growing out of its shoulders and back, and they menace foes. These snakes, however, are illusory and cannot do any harm.

0308 At a small shrine devoted to a saint prays a 4th-level cleric (ARMOR: plate + shield, HD 4, HP 10, MOVE 60'), garbed in a red surcoat with a white cross, and armed with a broad sword and a morning star. His riding horse stands nearby. The cleric is a horse-friend, and as such can communicate telepathically with any horse. All horses will obey him and show no fear at his bidding. Further, he can coax horses to safely run 50% farther and faster than the norm. Finally, horses under his influence will also have 50% more hit points.

0310 A 600 lb. clam (ARMOR: as plate + shield, HD 4, HP 14, MOVE 130' [walk], 1d10/two claws, 1d8/tail) stands 4' tall upon short, bird-like legs. Its emaciated humanoid arms end in sharp claws. The clam's body emits steam and even occasional jets of boiling water, and thus the clam takes only half damage from cold attacks. It can crawl along walls and ceilings as easily as upon the ground.

0310

0311 A four-legged roadrunner (ARMOR: as shield, HD 12, HP 51, MOVE 130', 1d8/slam) is man-sized and covered with sharp thorns. Its prehensile tongue is able to grab things up to 10' away. This monster is hit only by silver weapons. It charms opponents within a 10' radius, making those who fail their saving throws either

HEX DESCRIPTIONS

defend the monster or allow themselves to be eaten by it. Affected creatures receive a new saving throw at the end of each round.

0312 A beautiful monster (ARMOR: as leather + shield, HD 6, HP 21, MOVE 270' [fly], 90' [slither], 1d8/beak) has a 12' serpentine body covered with blue feathers, with the head and wings (10' span) of a blue jay.

0313 Water fills a cave in the sea cliff except at low tide. Therein a short, narrow passage leads up to a chamber (roughly spherical and 8' in diameter) that the water never reaches. On a natural rock pedestal sits a gold-plated wooden chalice which, if filled with holy water and drunk in a church, heals 3d8 HP. Any number of people can benefit, but each person can receive the healing only once on a given day.

0314 A statue of white stone (with a slight greenish tinge) depicts a smiling boy of about seven years of age. He holds out with his left hand a large rose which will spray poison on anyone who comes within its 5' range. The poison causes 15 points of damage unless a saving throw is made, in which case no damage is taken.

0315 The clouds of steam ascending from a statue can be seen five miles away. The 30' tall forged bronze statue depicts an athletic man. Its entire surface is unbearably hot to the touch.

0316 The waters of a gently rippling pool seem unremarkable, but anyone touching the water (unless a saving throw is made) will 1d4 hours later turn invisible and become immobile and unable to speak. This condition lasts for 24 hours. Water taken from the pool loses its magic within minutes.

0404 On the shore, a corked bottle of strange shape and hue contains a short message from a man to his

0311

0312

II

ISLE OF THE UNKNOWN

former love. They were to wed when he returned from his ocean voyage, which ended with a shipwreck, marooning him (the only survivor) upon an isle of the old pagan ecstasies, intoxicating and seductive. He obviously has shed few tears.

0405 Standing amidst the forest is a statue hewn from a deep nut-brown wood depicting an old woman with a kind and smiling face. Anyone who gently touches a hand of the statue will be granted for 1 month the insight to understand and the knowledge to speak with burrowing mammals. Any given person can obtain this power from the statue no more than once per year.

0406 A mentally unbalanced adolescent girl, disheveled and garbed in a torn and weathered tunic, wanders the land. She is a 4th-level magic-user (ARMOR: no armor, HD 4, HP 10, MOVE 120′, 1d4/dagger) with great powers of clairvoyance that wax and wane with the moon. When the moon is full, she can see nearly whatever and wherever she will. At the new moon her power fades almost to nothing.

0407 A 6′ tall roadrunner (ARMOR: as leather + shield, HD 8, HP 32, MOVE 120′, 1d6/beak, 1d4/tail) has glowing orange eyes which reduce its chance to surprise in the darkness to 1 in 6. This monstrosity can crawl upon walls and ceilings as swiftly as it can move upon the ground. It can project a 120′ diameter circle of poison (16 points damage per round, save for half) up to 90′ away. The creature can also spit with a range of 20′. Anyone hit by the spittle must make a saving throw or be stunned and unable to do anything for 1d8+1 rounds.

0408 A 150 lb. *Strombus* (ARMOR: as chain + shield, HD 1, HP 5, MOVE 140′ [fly only], 2d6/bash, 2d4/tail) inhabits an orange and pink conch shell 7′ long. The *Strombus* itself is albino with pink eyes. Any weapon

0407

12

HEX DESCRIPTIONS

0408

attack which rolls less than half of its maximum damage bounces off the conch shell, doing no damage. Missile weapons that bounce off the conch shell have a 5% chance of hitting a random being within 20' of the monster.

0408

ISLE OF THE UNKNOWN

0409 A huge, four-legged python (ARMOR: as chain, HD 13, HP 70, MOVE 130' [walking & flying], 1d12/bite) has two man-like arms. Most horribly, its skin is transparent. This serpent can shape-shift into any living creature, though it does not gain any magical powers in so doing. It takes only half damage from crushing attacks and from fire. It can charge into mêlée, doing double damage. If the snake bites, it latches on and automatically does 1d12 damage/round. When the monster's to hit score succeeds by 4 or more than necessary, its bite does an additional 1d6 damage, plus it makes a random limb useless for 1–20 days. In lieu of a mêlée attack, the python can dispel magic as a 13th-level magic-user, or it can spit in an opponent's eyes, randomly changing the opponent's alignment for 1d4 days (save avoids).

0410 A rumor is spreading through this town (population 1,500) that a detachment of men-at-arms is several days late in returning. The town's lord had sent out men to slay the horrid dragon (see hex 0409) that has plagued the town. Unfortunately, the men entered the cave in hex 0411.

0411 A narrow cave mouth will barely allow a man to squeeze through. The cave itself forms a rough corridor 5' in diameter that dead-ends after 40'. Those leaving the cave will find themselves in an identical cave in hex 2414. A given person can teleport between the caves only once in his life.

0412 A 7' tall lizard-man (ARMOR: as leather + shield, HD 10, HP 42, MOVE 120' [walk, fly, & swim], 1d10/two bites) has black crow's wings. It will attack any human it sees, concentrating on whomever currently has the fewest hit points. In lieu of its mêlée attacks, the lizard-man can shoot sharp scales (one per round) from its shoulders with a range of 50'. Those struck by a scale will lose 2 points of wisdom (no save). The lost points return at a rate of 1 per hour. Whenever

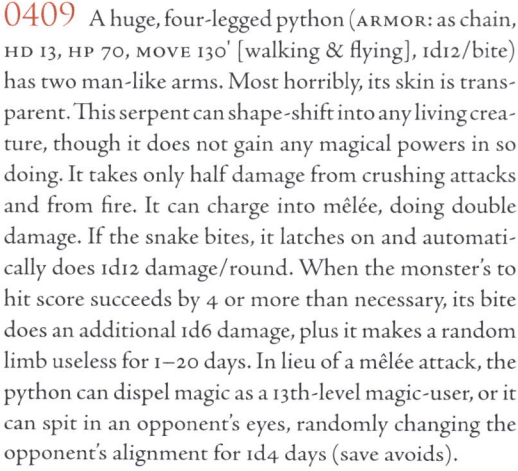

0409

Hex Descriptions

the creature is damaged (except by a spell), it separates into two creatures, each with the new lower hit point total and each acting independently, attacking the same target as the "full" creature did. The duplicates vanish when combat ends. In lieu of its mêlée attacks, the lizard-man can fire a paralysis ray from its eyes with a range of 30'. Those struck by it will be unable to move until a saving throw is made. (A saving throw is allowed each round.) The monster is immune to all magic that is not lightning-based. When taking damage from lightning the creature does not duplicate. In lieu of its mêlée attacks, the creature is able to make the metal equipment of one character become blazing hot. This attack can be centered on a point up to 120' away from the monster, affecting everyone within a 10' radius (save avoids). The metal equipment of those who fail the save heats up over a period of four rounds. The first round it merely gets warmer, giving victims a chance to discard it without harm. On the second round, if the character is still holding or wielding metal, he takes 1d6 damage. On the third round, he takes 1d8. On the fourth round, he takes 1d10. After that, the metal has cooled down enough to not cause further damage.

0413 A 7th-level cleric (ARMOR: plate + shield, HD 7, HP 35, MOVE 60') with eight 0-level men at arms (ARMOR: chain + shield, HP 1d6, HP 4, 5, 4, 5, 5, 4, 6, 6, MOVE 90') ride north. Dight with red surcoats emblazoned with white crosses, they seek diabolists to slay. They are armed with lances, broad swords, and daggers. When the cleric receives a wound, his companions in battle heal an identical number of hit points. For example, if the cleric loses 5 HP in battle, each man of his company will heal 5 HP (but no higher than each man's maximum HP).

0414 Here resides an Arabic 5th-level female magic-user (ARMOR: none, HD 5, HP 11, MOVE 120'). Though armed with scimitars and daggers, her magical ability

0412

to shapechange usually obviates their need. Within seconds, she can (without limitations) change herself into anything in the natural world: lion, fern, pearl, pool of water, mosquito, stone, etc.

0415 Large, sensuous roses of all hues (including the mysterious blue rose) grace a meadow. Those engulfed by their perfume will enjoy an ecstasy of incommunicable dreams. No discord of any sort is possible amongst the blossoms.

0416 Though one of the major towns (population 5,500) of the island, only a very few of the townsmen know of the secret meadow 6 miles away in hex 0415.

0503 Covered with the verdigris of age, a copper statue is of a crowned man holding aloft a trident in his right hand, while his left hand holds the reins of the four seahorses that pull his chariot. His gaze and his trident point toward the sea. Anyone who pricks his finger upon the trident will be able to command any creature of the sea for one hour. This gift must be used within one week.

0504 A pool of light blue water will teleport anyone who steps within it to a tarn of blue water in hex 1609. No saving throw applies. If a creature is teleported here from the tarn in 1609, he will not be able to magically teleport through the pool for 28 days.

0505 Each of eight 75 lb. porcupines (ARMOR: as leather, HD 9, HP 32, 37, 31, 51, 41, 42, 22, 49, MOVE 130' [swimming only], 1d6/bite) has four poisonous asps growing from its body instead of legs. Each round a porcupine itself bites, as does one of its asps (10 points of damage, save avoids). The gaze of a porcupine drains 1 point of strength (which returns at the rate of 1 point/hour). They can also shape-shift into swordfish, which doubles their movement rate.

HEX DESCRIPTIONS

0508

0506 This town (population 1,900) has its share of fishermen who swear that they have seen in the night a 100' long white shark swimming in the bay.

0507 All the animals that lair in the forest in this hex speak the common language of the island. Their intelligence is manlike. Such animals become dumb if taken outside the hex.

0508 In the midst of the woods stands a statue of a nude woman, her body partially obscured by her ankle-length hair. In the spring her skin is light golden in color, with honey-gold hair and green eyes. In the summer her skin is a deep golden, with platinum blonde hair and deep blue eyes. In autumn her skin is the color of delicate reddish-pink rose petals, with red hair and hazel eyes. In winter her skin is pale blue, with white hair and ice blue eyes.

0505

17

HEX DESCRIPTIONS

0509 Dandelions, carnations, and pinks dot the shady green sward beneath towering oak, birch, mulberry, chestnut, and ash trees. The number and variety of game animals make this a veritable Happy Hunting Ground. The lord of this forest is an 8th-level magic-user (ARMOR: none, HD 8, HP 45, MOVE 120') dressed in rich purple and dark blue hunting garb, sitting his red-brown horse bareback as though he were a part of it. He is a robust and jovial man of middle years with blue eyes and curling reddish hair and beard. He is armed with a short bow, a spear, and a dagger. He loves nothing so much as the hunt, save perhaps his dozen Scottish Deerhounds (ARMOR: none, HD 1+1, HP 2, 8, 6, 3, 6, 9, 3, 9, 8, 5, 3, 8, MOVE 180', 1d6/bite). The magic-user can speak with and understand all the animals of the forest, and he can communicate telepathically with his hounds anywhere within the forest. He can become invisible (though not during mêlée) and can move without sound.

0510 An ice cave high in the mountains holds four perfectly rectangular blocks of ice containing a *Smilodon*, a cave bear, a mammoth, and a dire wolf.

0511 A two-headed humanoid raven (ARMOR: as leather + shield, HD 1, HP 2, MOVE 240' [fly], 120' [walk], 1d6/bash) stands 6' tall. It can be surprised only 1 in 6. The raven-man attacks by buffeting foes with its wings.

0512 In the midst of an 80' diameter circle of icy ground stands an ice-carved image of an old, bearded man. Those coming within 40' of the image must make a saving throw each round or take 1d8 points of damage from the cold. Each of the eyes of the image is a colorless zircon (worth 50 g.p. each). These zircons, however, will always feel as cold as ice.

0511

ISLE OF THE UNKNOWN

0513 A dozen vividly-colored trout (two each of blue, green, yellow, orange, red, and purple) swim in a gently rippling clear amber pool. Anyone who eats a trout will gain or lose (50% chance of either) 1 point from a randomly-determined ability score. A saving throw applies (whether for weal or for woe), and the effect is permanent.

0514 An invisible statue casts a shadow. Tactile inspection reveals it to be a man carved from stone. If anyone attempts to damage the statue, it will animate (ARMOR: as plate + shield, HD 11, HP 50, MOVE 30', 2d6/blow) and attack while remaining invisible. Any man brought to 0 or fewer HP by the statue will not be killed but rather knocked unconscious. When he awakens, he will find that he is totally and permanently blind.

0515 A statue of gray stone depicts a figure with his countenance hidden by a hooded cloak. In his hands he holds an hourglass. If anyone approaches closer than 10' to the statue, it will boom forth in a sepulchral voice, "Touch not the glass, lest your present be altered." If anyone dares touch the hourglass, he will be transported back in time 1d10 centuries (save avoids). If anyone else touches the hourglass within the same hour, he too will be transported back in time to the same century to which the first time-traveler arrived. After more than an hour elapses, other time-travelers will probably be sent back to a different century.

0516 A tale is told in a tavern of this town (population 1,700) of a young, traveling monk who touched a statue north of town and disappeared (cf. hex 0515) before the eyes of his companions.

0602 An 8' tall humanoid swan (ARMOR: as leather, HD 10, HP 50, MOVE 240' [fly], 120' [walk & swim], 1d10+1/bite) has three "sleeping" human faces on the front of its torso. The monster has a +1 to initiative, and

0602

HEX DESCRIPTIONS

summoned monsters will absolutely refuse to attack it. Any creature attempting to attack the swan-man within 100′ of it will be charmed. A saving throw is allowed each round to break the charm. This creature can, once per round (but not during mêlée) shoot a feather up to 60′, which will drain its victim of 3 points of strength (which returns at the rate of 1 point per hour).

0603 This is one of the larger towns (population 5,300) of the island. A distraught young woman has told all her acquaintances that her lover disappeared before her very eyes when he jumped into a tarn (hex 0504).

0604 A 240 lb. mantis (ARMOR: as chain + shield, HD 3, HP 24, MOVE 120′, 1d6/forelegs, 1d12/bite) walks on its hind legs on walls and ceilings as easily as on floors. Its skin constantly throbs and bubbles. A successful attack with its spiked forelegs indicates that the mantis is holding its victim, thus automatically doing 1d6 damage each round.

0605 In the open sunshine glimmers the iridescent waters of a 10′ diameter pool. Any adventurer who drinks of it will change for 2d8 days to a randomly-determined class (no saving throw). Hit points might need to be re-rolled, spells might need to be randomly selected, etc. The character's six ability scores and level will remain unchanged. At the end of the 2d8 days, his previous class and characteristics will return. Drinking the waters while transformed will have no effect. The water loses its enchantment if taken from the pool for more than 1 hour.

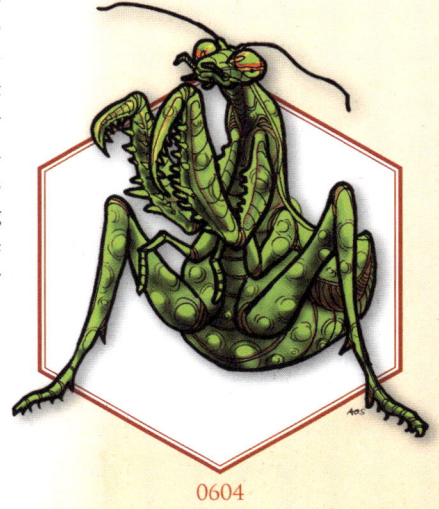

0604

HEX DESCRIPTIONS

0606 On a rocky cliff-side on the seashore is a 150' diameter cave lit from within by a light equal to sunlight, inside of which flourish pansies and ivy and a forest of pine, yew, willow, aspen, elm, and poplar. This is the home of a 7th-level magic-user (ARMOR: none, HD 7, HP 24, MOVE 120'), dressed in a gray dress and adorned with two bracelets of silver and turquoise (worth 400 g.p. each). She is the mistress of about 50 mountain goats (gray females and dark green males), the milk of which grants a +1 to all saving throws for 24 hours. The magic-user can transform into a mountain goat, and she can leap from the cliffs to turn into a barracuda to swim in the sea. If attacked she can make all her attackers within 150' feel as heavy as lead (no saving throw), and thus unable to attack.

0607 An ancient marble font (15' diameter) amongst aspen holds slightly dirty water. In the center of its 18" deep water is the illusion of a stone coffer roughly 1' square. Anything touching the illusion will pass through but not dispel it. Only while the waters are roughly roiled will the illusion vanish. Unlike the otherwise identical font in hex 1202, this font will not teleport anyone.

0608 Five hummingbirds (ARMOR: as leather, HD 12, HP 52, 51, 46, 45, 58, MOVE 190' [flying only], 1d4/beak) are the size of wolves, have feathered human-like arms, and a lizard-like fin runs down the center of their heads and backs. They are immune to lightning, only wooden or silver weapons can harm them, and crushing attacks cause them only half damage. Their gaze causes victims to uncontrollably dance for 1d4+1 rounds. Dancing characters cannot attack or cast spells, automatically fail all saving throws, cannot use shields, and suffer a 4 point penalty to armor. These monsters can project a cone of pale yellow light that causes confusion (save applies). A confused character will (25% chance of each) attack the nearest creature, stand perfectly still, run in a random direction, or attack an ally.

0608

HEX DESCRIPTIONS

0609 Tulips of variegated colors bloom in profusion in a meadow roughly 300' in diameter. When any human walks in the meadow, the stalks of the flowers bend towards the person, and a musical humming almost too soft to be heard emanates from the tulips.

0610 A 30' long serpentine platypus (ARMOR: as chain + shield, HD 5, HP 28, MOVE 120' [slithering or flying], 2d6/bash) has no limbs, so it slithers as a snake upon the ground, walls, or ceiling with equal facility. It copiously perspires blood. At will the beast can emit light (as the spell) from its body. Anyone killed by it will transform and rise as another such creature in 3d12 hours. A *Remove Curse* spell will restore such victims' humanity.

0611 In a secluded glen, perpetual spring reigns. Within grow bay laurel, palm, and apple trees. The vegetation is a veritable cornucopia of medicinal herbs and flowers. From one of the trees grows golden apples that when eaten cure all diseases and leave one in a drunken stupor for 12 hours. This valley is a paradise to all but ophidiophobics, for harmless snakes (brightly colored and gorgeously patterned) slither throughout. An 8th-level magic-user (ARMOR: none, HD 8, HP 31, MOVE 120') dwells here. He carries a 6' long snake, patterned with blue and yellow rings, across his shoulders. The magic-user is armed only with a bronze staff. He will use his medicinal knowledge of the valley's flora to heal all non-hostile men at a rate of 1d8 HP per day. The snakes here will attack in writhing hordes anyone wicked enough to harm the magic-user. Each victim will automatically take 1d6 points of damage each round until he escapes the valley.

0612 A mossy stone well stands 30' from the last remnants of a wooden cabin. The winch still works, and the wooden bucket is still sound. The dark green waters 20' down will lower a drinker's charisma by 1d6 points

0610

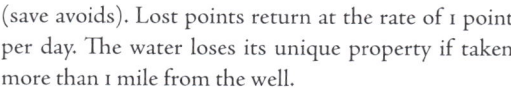

(save avoids). Lost points return at the rate of 1 point per day. The water loses its unique property if taken more than 1 mile from the well.

0613 A quadruped tawny eagle (ARMOR: none, HD 4, HP 21, MOVE 260′ [fly], 130′ [walk], 1d8+1/claw) is the size of a riding horse. Its body is completely covered with feathered human faces fixed in idiotic stares.

0614 A statue of a gowned woman is of dark gray stone veined with silver. The statue animates (ARMOR: as plate +shield, HD 10, HP 45, MOVE 60′, 5d4/breath) whenever touched by the light of the moon. Her breath weapon has a range of 10′, and it looks like pale moonlight. Anyone brought to 0 or fewer HP by her breath will turn into a moonbeam and vanish moonward.

0615 Rotted cypress trees lean against lichen-speckled temple ruins of white and purple marble. Fat chameleons crawl among the fallen pillars, crumbled walls, and broken stelae covered in bas-reliefs of various serpents and tropical birds. Six broken statues of goddesses lie amongst the rubbish.

0702 A 320 lb. turtle (ARMOR: as chain + shield, HD 4, HP 20, MOVE 90′ [walk and swim], 2d8/bite) bites with spike-like teeth. Because its body continually sheds water, the monster takes only half damage from heat-based attacks.

0703 A bronze-haired nude woman of sultry beauty stands chained to a rock. She wears a golden necklace (worth 600 g.p.). She will coyly promise a great reward for those who courteously free her, and a correspondingly great punishment for those who do not free her or who treat her roughly. The reward is an increase of 6 experience levels, one of which disappears with each passing day. The curse is the loss of 6

0702

HEX DESCRIPTIONS

0703

experience levels (save avoids, and no one will drop below 0 level), one of which returns with each passing day. The woman vanishes as soon as she bestows boon or bane.

0613

ISLE OF THE UNKNOWN

0704 Near the shore grow pear and peach trees as well as orchids and goldenrod. Here wanders a 7th-level magic-user (ARMOR: as chain, HD 7, HP 18, MOVE 90') in an electric blue tunic and armed only with a harpoon. He always carries a large aluminum jar. Any water in the jar comes under the magic-user's dominion. It can, according to his whim, heal 2d8 points of damage per draught, or it can shoot from the jar with such force as to knock anyone down it hits, or reach out with drowning tentacles that do 2d8 points of damage per round (save for half damage), or form a pillar of water to bear the magic-user aloft, etc. The jar is not enchanted in anyone else's hands. He can also communicate with and command seagulls. Upon his right hand is a silver ring set with a polished and cut aquamarine (worth 1,000 g.p.).

0705 A statue of a smiling and handsome young man is carved of polished obsidian. Its eyes are blacker than black, and if anyone studies the statue's face within 5', he will feel engulfed within the ultra-blackness of the eyes (unless a saving throw is made). Such victims become paralyzed and take 1d12 points of damage each round, with a new saving throw made each round. If the victim is pulled away, the statue will animate (ARMOR: as plate + shield, HD 13, HP 59, MOVE 60', 4d8/scythe) and attack with a scythe magically appearing in its hands.

0706 A strawberry bush growing alone in a clearing buds in the fall, bears succulent fruit in the winter, shrivels in the spring, and goes dormant in the summer.

0707 High in the mountains is an icy blue pool (30' diameter) fed from the runoff of melting snow. Anyone who drinks the bracing waters will have 1 point added to his wisdom for 2d8 days. The water loses all its enchantment if taken more than 12' from the pool.

ISLE OF THE UNKNOWN

0708

0708 A 16' tall aspen (ARMOR: none, HD 9, HP 41, MOVE none, 1d8/bash) has four trunks rising from the ground to join into a larger trunk 6' above the ground. One of the four lower trunks has the likeness of an ineffably sad human face, while the opposite one has the likeness of a laughing human face. Anyone who dares to touch one of the faces (or who damages the tree) will be buffeted by a branch of the aspen tree.

0709 Thirteen bipedal termites (ARMOR: as chain + shield, HD 7, HP 32, 32, 19, 30, 32, 36, 29, 35, 32, 26, 26, 32, 48, MOVE 90', 1d3/projectile) are 2' tall, have glowing blue eyes, and are covered with sores oozing foul slime. Anyone touching the ooze will lose 3 points of strength (which return at the rate of 1 point/hour). The gaze of a termite-man will trap its victim in a crackling blue energy barrier of up to 35 square feet. Those trapped are helpless, but another can harmlessly collapse the barrier by touching it with metal. The monsters attack by spurting (up to 40' distant) a noxious liquid. They can walk upon walls and ceilings.

0710 Upon a sweeping greensward rises a castle invisible to all those outside it. To those entering the castle, though, it becomes visible. Here dwells a grave and courteous knight, who is a 5th-level fighter (ARMOR: plate + shield, HD 5, HP 24, MOVE 60'), and his retinue of 40 souls.

0711 A 7' long caterpillar (ARMOR: as plate + shield, HD 6, HP 23, MOVE 120', 1d6+1/bite) has skin made of metal. It can crawl upon walls and ceilings as easily as upon the ground.

0712 A woodcutter from this town (population 1,800) claims to have found a glen of perpetual spring (hex 0611). His fear of the multitudinous serpents within the glen kept him from entering.

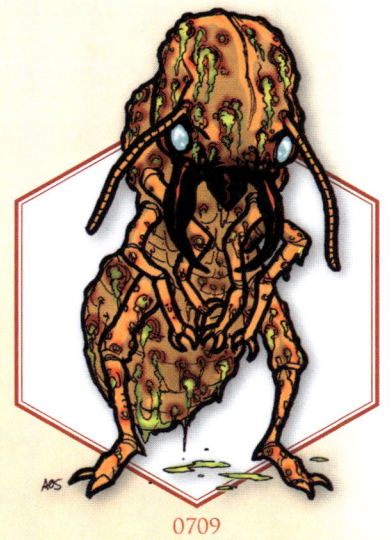

0709

HEX DESCRIPTIONS

0713 The delicate influence of the Enchantress of Petals, a 6th-level magic-user (ARMOR: none, HD 6, HP 10, MOVE 120'), keeps winter and autumn at bay in this secluded mountain vale. Garbed in dresses made of flower petals, her fresh and tender beauty makes it impossible to attack her unless a saving throw is made at −3. She can entice flowers of any sort to grow to maturity within minutes, and she can make animated rose bushes with long thorns to both defend and attack (automatic 1d6 damage per round, no saving throw).

0714 Twelve weird monstrosities (ARMOR: none, HD 5, HP 22, 23, 27, 27, 27, 23, 22, 21, 20, 18, 27, 18, MOVE 60', 1d3/fists) consist of transparent mold in the shape of 18" tall humanoids. They are so unnatural that they cannot abide the existence of humans (though any magically affected human [cursed, polymorphed, etc.] will not be attacked by the creatures except in self-defense). In combat each will attack the foe that inflicted the most damage with its most recent attack. Failing that, they will attack the foe with the most remaining hit points. In mêlée these creatures are quite ineffective, flailing with their small fists. In lieu of its mêlée attack, these monsters can generate a circle of death. Any creature within this area must make a saving throw or take 3d10 points of damage each round it is in the area of effect. This attack can be centered on a point up to 70' away from the monster, affecting everyone within a 70' radius. These mold-men are unable to be hurt by fire (whether natural or magical).

0715 Amongst the pines is the humble home of the Chromatic Master of Hues, a 4th-level magic-user (ARMOR: chain, HD 4, HP 10, MOVE 90') armed with a halberd with a multi-colored shaft. His only power is the ability to change the color of anything in his sight (no saving throw). He will change the color of any man who threatens him. Hot pink skin with bright yellow

0711

0714

polka-dots is a favorite. Who would wish to go through life so?

0716 A life-sized statue of ivory of the purest white is of a Grecian philosopher. On clear nights, the statue animates upon the appearance of the first actual star (the Evening Star and other planets do not count), returning to statue form with the fleeing of the last star (again, not counting the Morning Star or any other planet). With a clear and serene intellect, the animated statue will speak expertly and indefatigably on all matters sidereal. If anyone attacks the statue, it will typically turn invisible and silently walk away. If pressed, the statue is a fearful opponent (ARMOR: as plate + shield, HD 12, HP 54, MOVE 60', 4d6/fist). It is immune to all magic.

0802 In a cavern in the rocky shore, a worn 4' by 5' Turkish tapestry with geometric designs (worth 20 g.p.) enfolds a conch shell. Both items have been dedicated to diabolic rites. When blown, the conch makes a discordant braying. Anyone sounding it will have a −1 penalty to all saving throws and to hit and damage rolls for the next 24 hours (save avoids).

0803 This monster (ARMOR: as chain + shield, HD 6, HP 27, MOVE 40' [crawl], 80' [fly], 1d10/bite) is a 10' long lizard with large, white crane wings and suction cups on its limbs that allow it to crawl along walls and ceilings as swiftly as on the ground. This giant lizard attacks all humans with a vicious bite. It will attack spellcasters (magic-users before clerics) before anyone else. If no spellcasters are present, it will attack the foe with the fewest remaining hit points. The creature is surprised only 1 in 12.

0804 A statue on an unknown, blue-gray metal depicts a sardonically smiling man of gaunt countenance. On his outstretched right forearm are seven beetles of

HEX DESCRIPTIONS

0804

the same mysterious metal. If someone's hand comes within several inches of the beetles, they will shrilly chitter. A person who touches a beetle will be attacked the next time he sleeps by a swarm of multifarious beetles that arise out of the ground. The victim will take 1d4 points of damage per round. He can escape from the slow-moving swarm and brush the attacking insects off of himself in 3 rounds. Immersion in water will also stop the damage.

0803

ISLE OF THE UNKNOWN

0805 A life-sized statue of a smiling young man, hewn of a bright yellow stone, has two songbirds perched upon his outstretched hand. Those who touch the statue will understand the language of birds for the next fortnight. Any such who harms a bird within that fortnight will lose this magical ability and will be subject to frequent attack by birds of all types during the fortnight.

0806 This 200 lb. white rabbit (ARMOR: as leather, HD 2, HP 8, MOVE 130', 1d6+1/claw) is immune to blunt weapons, and it attacks with its long claws on its front feet.

0807 In an ice cave above tree line is the abode of the Ice Wizard, a 6th-level magic-user (ARMOR: none, HD 6, HP 18, MOVE 120'). He can cause each round 1d4+1 giant icicles to fall upon opponents for 3d6 points of damage each (save for half damage). When an attack of whatever sort succeeds against him, the Ice Wizard can avoid all damage from it (75 % chance of success) by creating an icy barrier between himself and the blow.

0808 A wavering green light dimly illumines a humid grotto, roughly a 20' sphere. Brightly colored oceanic fish "swim" through the air, and aquatic plants gently sway to invisible currents.

0809 A 6th-level cleric (ARMOR: plate + shield, HD 6, HP 23, MOVE 60') armed with mace, spear, and long bow (with 30 arrows) wears a red surcoat emblazoned with a white cross. He possesses the miraculous gift of never missing with a weapon. His riding horse crops the grass nearby. The head of the cleric's order has given him a secret mission to perform.

0810 A huge amoeba (ARMOR: as plate, HD 6, HP 29, MOVE 120', 1d10/touch) is about 9' long and 6' wide. Its surface looks like the black and yellow mottled skin of a

0810

Hex Descriptions

wet salamander. A salamander-like head forms from its bulk in order to eat. Weapons tend to bounce off of its rubbery body, and thus they do only half damage. This blob's touch is both poisonous (16 points damage, save at −2 for half) and causes a disease (requiring a second save with no penalty) that is fatal in 2d10 days.

0811 In an unnaturally and perpetually shaded copse stands a pale green statue of an emaciated old man blowing a horn. If anyone comes within 10′ of the statue, it will speak in a harsh whisper, "Touch not the horn." On closer approach, the statue will again warn, "Your regret will be great if you dare touch the horn." If the horn is nevertheless touched, a plague will fall upon the nearby town in hex 0812, with 10 % of the populace dying within three days. Chances are that the townsmen will discover whose irresponsibility brought doom upon them, making a trip to town quite interesting.

0812 The people of this town (population 1,500) shun the copse in hex 0811 out of hereditary fear, though they know not the reason for their dread. They will seek to dissuade anyone who proposes to travel to the copse.

ISLE OF THE UNKNOWN

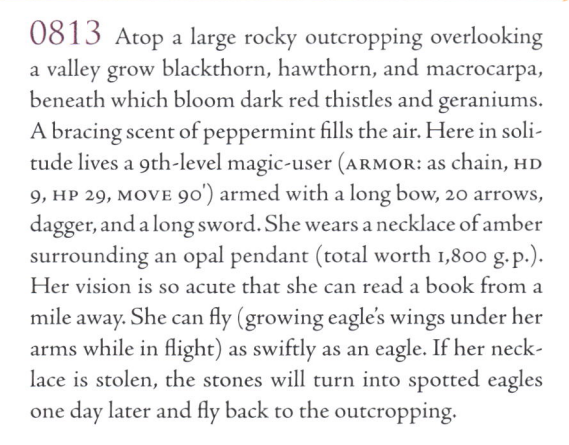

0813 Atop a large rocky outcropping overlooking a valley grow blackthorn, hawthorn, and macrocarpa, beneath which bloom dark red thistles and geraniums. A bracing scent of peppermint fills the air. Here in solitude lives a 9th-level magic-user (ARMOR: as chain, HD 9, HP 29, MOVE 90′) armed with a long bow, 20 arrows, dagger, and a long sword. She wears a necklace of amber surrounding an opal pendant (total worth 1,800 g.p.). Her vision is so acute that she can read a book from a mile away. She can fly (growing eagle's wings under her arms while in flight) as swiftly as an eagle. If her necklace is stolen, the stones will turn into spotted eagles one day later and fly back to the outcropping.

0814 Seven crows (ARMOR: as shield, HD 6, HP 27, 28, 31, 23, 27, 29, 30, MOVE 130′ [levitation], 1d6/blade) can move only by levitating, and as such can never be more than 10′ from a solid surface. They have four legs, each terminating in a razor-sharp blade. When a crow successfully hits with a roll of 18 or higher, the victim must make a saving throw or lose the use of a random limb for 1 hour. These monsters have a +6 bonus to all their saving throws.

0815 Deep in the shadows of the forest lives an old hermit, a 10th-level cleric (ARMOR: none, HD 9+2, HP 24, MOVE 120′) who has withdrawn from the company of men to live a life of prayer and holiness. In a trunk in his rude hovel he keeps his plate armor, shield, long sword, war hammer, and red surcoat with a white cross. This kindly man will use forest herbs to heal any man in need who comes to his door. A person under his care will heal 1d12 HP/day, and blindness, disease, etc. will be cured at once.

0816 A red statue of a bearded warrior holds a broad sword and is fully armored with helm, shield, and armor of red scales. The red scale armor is not a part of the statue, but an actual suit of armor worn

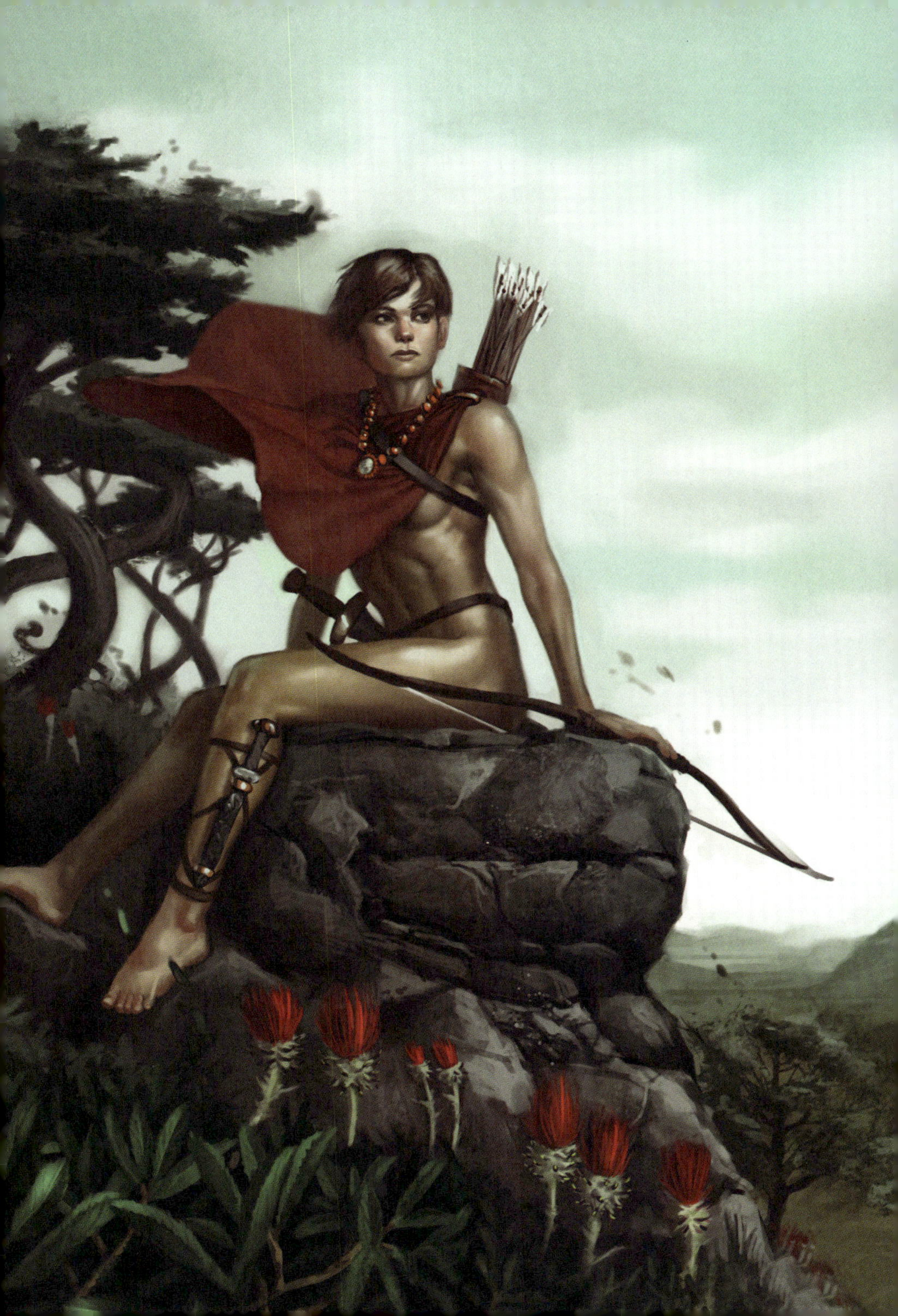

by it. If anyone attempts to take the armor, the statue will animate (ARMOR: as plate + shield, HD 15, HP 68, MOVE 60', 2d8/sword) and forbid the taking of the armor. Anyone wearing the armor (which gives an armor equal to plate) will be immune to the fires of the pillar in hex 2009. Perhaps unsurprisingly, no one through all the ages has discovered that the statue will gladly give the armor to one who asks nicely for it using the magic word: Please.

0902 A statue of cream-colored stone depicts a stunningly beautiful woman clothed only in her knee-length, honey-gold hair. So bewitching is the statue that no human can possibly bring himself to do it harm. Those who fail a saving throw will gently caress the statue, and when night falls the statue will animate and spend sweet hours with such unfortunates, who thereby gladly lose 1d8 HP. The next day her victims must make another saving throw at −1 or fall into the same trap. Each day thereafter the saving throw is more difficult (−2, −3, etc.). In case a non-human attacks the statue, it animates (ARMOR: as plate + shield, HD 12, HP 54, MOVE 30', 3d4/constriction) and its hair attacks like a constrictor snake, automatically doing damage each round after a hit (up to two opponents at once).

0903 Many of the people of this town (population 2,800) fear the coastline in hex 0802 because of its reputation for diabolism and great sea worms.

0904 A statue of weathered gray stone depicts a man with a snake body below the waist and three heads: man, bull, and lion. If someone approaches within 10' of the statue, the man's head will say, "One, and only one, may touch a single brow. Two bring weal, but one brings woe. Choose well, or approach not." He who touches the man's head will gain a point of both intelligence and of wisdom. He who touches the bull's head will gain a point of both strength and of consti-

HEX DESCRIPTIONS

0906

tution. He who touches the lion's head will lose one point each of strength, constitution, and dexterity. The statue will not function again until after the next total solar eclipse.

0905 Four limbless, serpentine beavers (ARMOR: as leather + shield, HD 8, HP 45, 42, 35, 44, MOVE 60' [walk and swim], 1d6/tail) are the size of wolves, and they slither and swim in a jerky, unpredictable manner.

0906 A statue of silver depicts a nude woman with eagle's feet and wings. She has a long covering of feathers in place of hair. The statue will animate (ARMOR: as plate + shield, HD 10, HP 45, 120' [fly], 60' [walk], 5d8/screech) if molested and soar aloft, screeching each round so loudly that everyone within 100' takes 5d8 points of damage (save for half).

0905

39

ISLE OF THE UNKNOWN

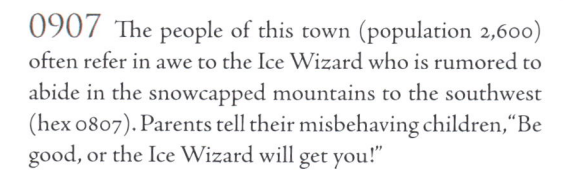

0907 The people of this town (population 2,600) often refer in awe to the Ice Wizard who is rumored to abide in the snowcapped mountains to the southwest (hex 0807). Parents tell their misbehaving children, "Be good, or the Ice Wizard will get you!"

0908 Boulders dot the pine forest. Those who look closely will see that the boulders possess rough, unhewn faces that move and twist as travelers go by.

0909 In the midst of a meadow (flower-filled in the spring and summer) a white marble statue of a chaste and demure maiden has a simple dress painted green. Her arms are fashioned as though cradling a baby. If a bunch of the meadow's flowers are placed in her arms and then boiled, it will make a tea that heals 3d6 points of damage (up to once each day). The tea loses its efficacy when taken from the meadow.

0910 A statue of wood-hued stone depicts a man holding a hammer and a needle, bending over an empty table. Any damaged mundane item placed upon the table will cause the statue to animate and repair the item as swiftly as could an expert craftsman of the most consummate skill.

0911 A statue of stone the color of golden honey depicts a beautiful nude woman reaching forth her right hand. The statue's eyes are polished sapphires. Anyone who tries to harm the statue will fall unconscious for 1d4+1 rounds (no saving throw) upon touching it. Any lawful and good character who touches his head to her right hand will be healed of all wounds.

0912 Eight 4' tall tailed and genderless humanoids (ARMOR: as chain, HD 3, HP 16, 9, 21, 15, 3, 23, 8, 15, MOVE 120', 1d6/bite, 1d6/tail) have rainbow skin, prismatic eyes, and mixed blue, pink, and green hair. They have the intelligence of gorillas.

HEX DESCRIPTIONS

0913 In the midst of a sedgy meadow stands a statue of blood-red stone depicting a smirking nude harlot. Those looking upon the statue must make a saving throw or become so obsessed with the statue that they must view her again the next day, at which time another saving throw must be rolled. Failure indicates that current hit points are reduced by half, and the statue must be viewed again that very night and a third saving throw rolled. If this saving throw is failed, the victim dies, his body drained of all blood.

0914 The eyes of a bear-sized, four-legged owl (ARMOR: as leather, HD 6, HP 17, MOVE 210' [fly], 130' [walk], 1d10/beak) are set on the ends of 4' long, mobile stalks. This greater range of vision makes the monster less likely to be surprised (1 in 6 chance).

0915 Choirs of multifarious songbirds impossibly sing symphonies worthy of Mozart. Anyone who fails a saving throw at +3 will throw himself down upon the soft grass for an hour's enjoyment of the music.

0916 Standing on an 80' diameter island in the midst of the river is a 10' tall green-blue statue of a bearded man with a fish tail. He holds a trident in his hands. Any who attempt to cross the river in any manner other than swimming will incur the statue's wrath, causing it to animate (ARMOR: as plate + shield, HD 14, HP 63, MOVE 120' [water], 40' [land], 3d6/trident) and swim to the attack.

1001 A two-headed quadruped pigeon (ARMOR: as shield, HD 2, HP 10, MOVE 130' [swim only], 1d6/two beaks) is the size of a Shetland pony and has bright blue plumage. It can be surprised only 1 in 6. This monster never leaves the water.

ISLE OF THE UNKNOWN

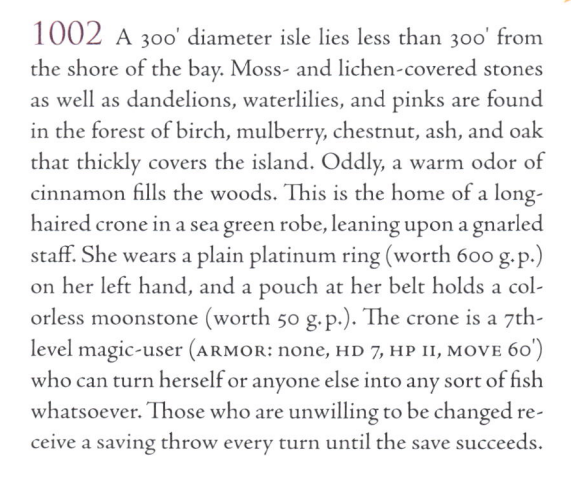

1002 A 300' diameter isle lies less than 300' from the shore of the bay. Moss- and lichen-covered stones as well as dandelions, waterlilies, and pinks are found in the forest of birch, mulberry, chestnut, ash, and oak that thickly covers the island. Oddly, a warm odor of cinnamon fills the woods. This is the home of a long-haired crone in a sea green robe, leaning upon a gnarled staff. She wears a plain platinum ring (worth 600 g.p.) on her left hand, and a pouch at her belt holds a colorless moonstone (worth 50 g.p.). The crone is a 7th-level magic-user (ARMOR: none, HD 7, HP 11, MOVE 60') who can turn herself or anyone else into any sort of fish whatsoever. Those who are unwilling to be changed receive a saving throw every turn until the save succeeds.

1003 A white marble statue depicts a 24' tall robed woman holding a sword in her right hand and a two pan balance in her left. If any person who is not of unswerving goodness and justice places himself on the right-hand scale, he will be transported to a random hex on the island. If he places himself on the left-hand scale, the statue will animate (ARMOR: as plate + shield, HD 12, HP 54, MOVE 40', 5d6/sword) and attack. If a just man places himself on the right-hand scale, he will receive a +2 bonus on all his saving throws for 1 month. If he places himself on the left-hand scale, all his wounds, diseases, infirmities, etc. will be cured.

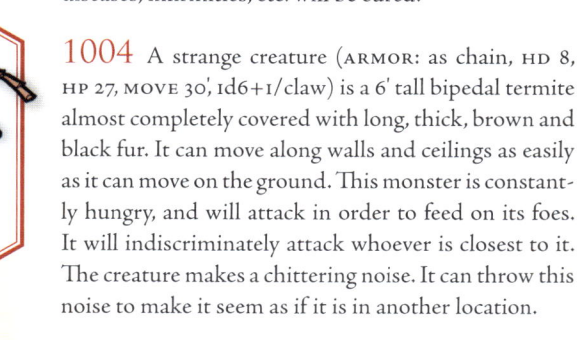

1004 A strange creature (ARMOR: as chain, HD 8, HP 27, MOVE 30', 1d6+1/claw) is a 6' tall bipedal termite almost completely covered with long, thick, brown and black fur. It can move along walls and ceilings as easily as it can move on the ground. This monster is constantly hungry, and will attack in order to feed on its foes. It will indiscriminately attack whoever is closest to it. The creature makes a chittering noise. It can throw this noise to make it seem as if it is in another location.

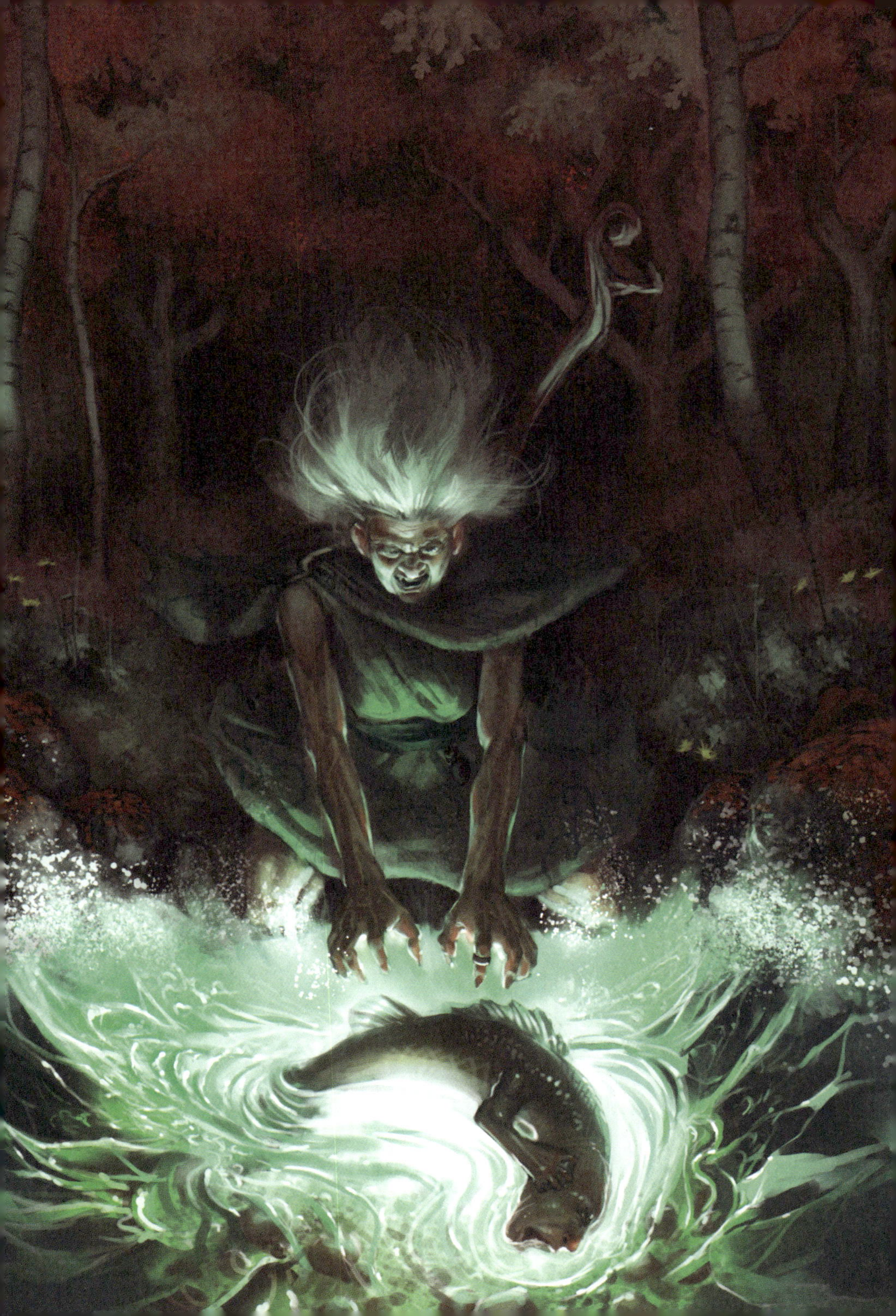

1005 Long ago the limpid waters of this secluded high-mountain tarn were blessed by a wandering saint. Ever since, the virtuous who drink the water will not thirst again for seven days. The waters lose their holiness if taken more than 49' from the tarn.

1006 A lone tower is the domicile of the Alchemist, an elderly 3rd-level magic-user (ARMOR: none, HD 3, HP 13, MOVE 120'). His castle is given over to laboratories crowded with aludels, crucibles, athanors, alembics, vats, cupels, furnaces, matrasses, etc. In his seekings after purification, enlightenment, and spiritualization, the Alchemist has discovered a fume that will restore one year of youth to those who are lawful, pious, and good. As the fume is efficacious only once each year, it will basically keep a righteous man from further aging.

1007 A stone obelisk lies almost entirely buried. Hieroglyphs cover one of the buried sides. Translated, they read, "The horse-head fire that burns in the watery abyss," which is the answer to a long-forgotten riddle.

1008 The opaque waters of six yellow tarns (each about 50' in diameter) will ripple if anyone approaches within 5' of them. Golden fish swim in the waters, which reach a depth of 30'. Pale violet-capped, colorless fungi up to 3' in height swell from the soil around the tarns. Anyone eating the fungus will suffer 10 points of damage (save for half) from the poison.

1009 A 3' diameter amoeba (ARMOR: none, HD 2, HP 4, MOVE 90' [slithering], 30' [tunneling], 1d10/caustic touch) is splotched white and gray. It lives in 3' tunnels that it has burrowed. Once per turn the amoeba can spew up to 10' a viscous slime (white and gray) that can form a barrier of 10 square feet. Anyone touching this barrier suffers 2d4 points of damage (save for half damage) per round while in contact with it. Flame readily destroys the barrier. This monster can turn itself into

HEX DESCRIPTIONS

a shadow, becoming in effect invisible. In this form it surprises 5 in 6, though it cannot attack or be attacked by non-magical means.

1010 Upon an inaccessible outcropping of rock high upon a mountainside is a statue of pure white marble depicting an armored warrior bearing a lance, seated upon a winged horse. Anyone who bloodies his hand upon the tip of the lance will gain a +3 to hit and damage, along with a +3 to saving throws, the next time he is in combat against a flying opponent.

1011 Scrub oaks shade a stream-fed pool (about 15' in diameter) of rippling amber water. Any magic-user or cleric who drinks of it loses all spell-casting abilities for one day, but during that same time his constitution, dexterity, and strength all rise to 18. The water loses its enchantment after one hour if taken from the pool.

1012 In a cheerful log cabin of naked pine lives a 2nd-level cleric (ARMOR: plate + shield, HD 2, HP 9, MOVE 60') with his seven fair daughters, each named for a virtue. When going into combat the cleric wears his red surcoat with a white cross, and he fights with a battle axe. Anyone attempting to harm or corrupt his daughters will turn into a songbird (no saving throw) for one day. If a wretch attempts this crime a second time, his transformation into a songbird will be permanent.

1013 A double-trunked saguaro cactus (ARMOR: none, HD 4, HP 11, MOVE none, 1d8/projectile thorns) stands 11' tall, and flames perpetually enshroud it. Anyone coming into contact with this plant takes damage equal to a splash of burning oil. The cactus will shoot its flaming thorns at anything coming within range (equal to a short bow).

ISLE OF THE UNKNOWN

1014 A disgusting heap (ARMOR: none, HD 9, HP 43, MOVE 10', 1d8/envelop) looks like a 7' diameter mass of pulped vines. It is immune to both mind-affecting magic and cold, and it is surprised only 1 chance in 6. A successful attack indicates that it has trapped its victim within its horrid bulk, thereafter automatically dealing 1d8 points of damage per round. Bizarrely, this monster can change into the shape of any living thing (without gaining any of its magical abilities).

1015 A statue of a barbarian is carved from a brownish green rock that has a blue sheen in the sunlight. Its eyes are set with wine-red garnet crystals (worth 100 g.p. each). If anyone attempts to take the garnets, the statue animates and attacks (ARMOR: as plate + shield, HD 11, HP 50, MOVE 30', 3d6/two fists). It regenerates 3 hp/round.

1016 This weird being (ARMOR: none, HD 4, HP 20, MOVE 30' [walk & swim], 1d6/slam) is a 6' tall humanoid blue jay. Its plumage is bright yellow in the crest, back, wings, and tail, and its face is blue. The underside is blue and the neck is collared with black which extends to the sides of the head. The wing primaries and tail are strongly barred with black, yellow, and blue. The bill, legs, and eyes are all black. While this monster cannot fly, it uses its wings to bash opponents. It attacks a randomly-determined foe each round out of sheer, constant hunger.

1101 This statue is of a long-haired woman with a long, billowing dress, all carved from pale blue crystal. Those who gaze long at the statue will seem to hear a gentle susurrus, and will seem to see the statue's dress ripple. If anyone attempts to harm the statue, a violent gust of wind will blow the person 30' away, doing 4d6 points of damage (save for half damage).

1102 Mirror-bright silver coats a statue of a nude youth wearing a winged petasos. Once per day, a person

Hex Descriptions

can whisper a message (no more than 100 words) into the statue's ear, and the message will be heard by any single person of the whisperer's choosing. The delivery of the message is delayed 1 minute for every mile between the statue and the intended recipient.

1103 A statue of blue-gray stone depicts a nude woman with eagle wings outstretched, her arms and countenance raised to the heavens. She animates (ARMOR: as plate + shield, HD 11, HP 50, MOVE 120' [fly], 90' [walk]) during any rainfall or thunderstorm, flying with exultation through the elements. She will call down lightning bolts (10d6 damage, save for half) on any who attempt to interfere with her while animated. If someone tries to damage or move the statue while not animated, he will receive an electrical shock for 6d6 damage (save for half).

1104 Regardless of the temperature, filming ice covers the ithyphallic runes covering the nine cracked and broken columns protruding from the ground. The runes describe in poetic terms the movements of the planets millennia ago.

1105 A 300 lb. koala (ARMOR: as leather, HD 14, HP 58, MOVE 130', 1d8+1/claw) has suction cups on it limbs, allowing it to move on walls and ceilings. Though wingless, it can also fly. The koala can be hit only by silver weapons. Bludgeoning weapons cause no damage, while cutting attacks cause half damage. Further, any weapon hitting the beast sticks to it. Such a weapon can be wrenched free only with a successful Open Doors roll (one attempt per round). This creature also regenerates 2 hp/round. It can hear absolutely everything within 50', and it can generate a 20' radius sphere of darkness. Finally, the koala can animate non-living objects (up to 70 cubic feet), causing them to attack (as 14 HD monsters). Damage and armor class varies according to the object, though in no case causing more than 20 points of damage with a single attack.

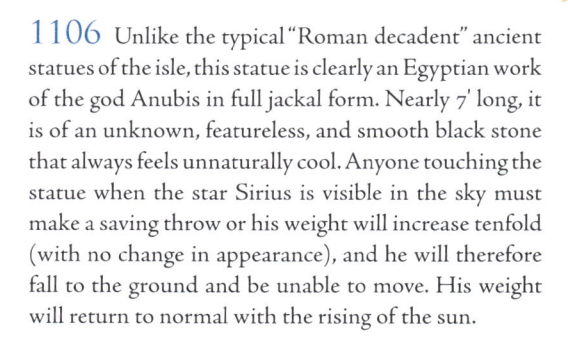

1106 Unlike the typical "Roman decadent" ancient statues of the isle, this statue is clearly an Egyptian work of the god Anubis in full jackal form. Nearly 7′ long, it is of an unknown, featureless, and smooth black stone that always feels unnaturally cool. Anyone touching the statue when the star Sirius is visible in the sky must make a saving throw or his weight will increase tenfold (with no change in appearance), and he will therefore fall to the ground and be unable to move. His weight will return to normal with the rising of the sun.

1107 Anyone touching this silver-coated statue of a man will receive an electrical shock doing 3d6 points of damage (save for half). During thunderstorms the statue animates (ARMOR: as plate + shield, HD 11, HP 50, MOVE 240′, 6d6/lightning) and calls lightning bolts down on everyone he sees (save for half damage).

1108 A cracked, ancient bench made of rosy-white marble rests in the shade of the forest. Anyone sitting upon it will be instantly transported 4d10 miles in a random direction (no saving throw).

1109 Seven monks reside in a small monastery. Known only to the abbot, the library thereof includes a delicate scroll inscribed with an unknown dialogue of Plato ("The Charalampos") on the mystical philosophy of number. The right buyer would pay thousands of gold pieces to acquire it.

1110 A statue of a beautiful nude woman is made from a translucent, icy blue stone. Once per day, the statue will accurately point in the exact direction (as the eagle flies) of any location, person, or object that the questioner seeks.

1111 An 8′ tall monster (ARMOR: as leather + shield, HD 2, HP 8, MOVE 30′, 1d10/bite) has the head and body of a snake with humanoid arms and legs. Its hide

HEX DESCRIPTIONS

reflects light in a way similar to an oil/water mixture, with shifting, kaleidoscope-like colors. The snake-man is fiercely territorial, and it considers anyone entering its cave to be a threat. The creature will not pursue any fleeing enemies outside its cave. In combat it prefers to attack the most heavily armored foe, followed by attacking the foe with the fewest remaining hit points.

1112 A 6' tall cockroach (ARMOR: as leather + shield, HD 9, HP 32, MOVE 120' [fly and walk], 1d6/bite, 1d6/projectile) walks upon its hind legs, and it can also do so upon walls and ceilings. The monster also has two octopoid tentacles with which it can grab and hold its victims. Such held victims can free themselves only with an open doors roll, and they can be automatically bitten each round. The cockroach's bite would be harmless but for its caustic spittle, which it can spew as far as a short bow.

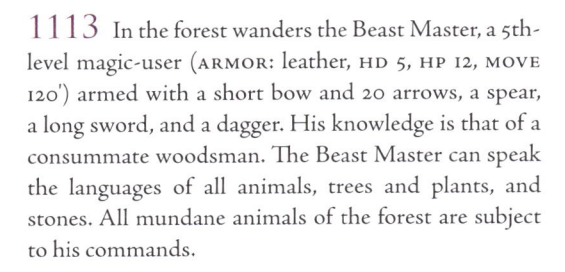

1113 In the forest wanders the Beast Master, a 5th-level magic-user (ARMOR: leather, HD 5, HP 12, MOVE 120') armed with a short bow and 20 arrows, a spear, a long sword, and a dagger. His knowledge is that of a consummate woodsman. The Beast Master can speak the languages of all animals, trees and plants, and stones. All mundane animals of the forest are subject to his commands.

1114 A 150 lb. monster (ARMOR: none, HD 5, HP 28, MOVE 120', 1d6+1/two claws) is a multi-colored (though primarily green) parrot with a lizard-like fin across its head and back, and four legs. It can neither fly nor walk, but moves by swift leaps. It moves its full movement rate but is in contact with the ground only at the very beginning and very end of its movement, as well as any point at which it turns. This creature is so unnatural that it cannot abide the existence of natural beings. It will attack whichever such being is closest to it. Any magically affected (cursed, polymorphed, etc.)

character will not be attacked by the creature except in self-defense. The creature regains 2 hit points at the beginning of every round, even after reaching 0 HP or lower. Acid, however, will cause it damage that does not regenerate.

1115 An Elysian garden of violets, large roses, foxgloves, daisies, and vines is dotted with cypress and ash trees. Copper and bronze statues of Classic Greek workmanship (as distinct from the late Roman statues typical of the island) stand throughout. Harmless lizards and small snakes make themselves at home. On a copper bench beneath a cypress tree sits a muscular and beardless young man in a pale green tunic intently contemplating a balance scale made of chrysolite, held aloft in his right hand. Close observation will reveal small beetles on the left pan of the scale. The man will ignore any visitors. Only at night does his concentration leave the scales to rise to the stars. If disturbed, he will (once only) say, "Beware, lest thou be weighed." Further disturbance (or if he is attacked) will make this 9th-level magic-user (ARMOR: none, HD 9, HP 23, MOVE 120') stand as his eyes blaze with crackling blue-green light which each round flashes upon all his attackers whom he can see. Such unfortunates must make a saving throw or be shrunk (along with all equipment) to a fraction of an inch tall and teleported onto the left pan of the magic-user's scales. The beetles thereon will now be, relatively speaking, giant beetles. If your game rules have statistics for giant beetles, use those. Assume 1d6 beetles of random type for each teleported character. Otherwise, you might consider giving the beetles ARMOR: as chain + shield, HD 2 to 12, MOVE 90', damage from 1d8 to 4d8. If the magic-user is slain, his scales will shatter with a great flare, with everyone returned to normal size. In this event 1d6 beetles have a 50 % chance of being transformed into actual giant beetles.

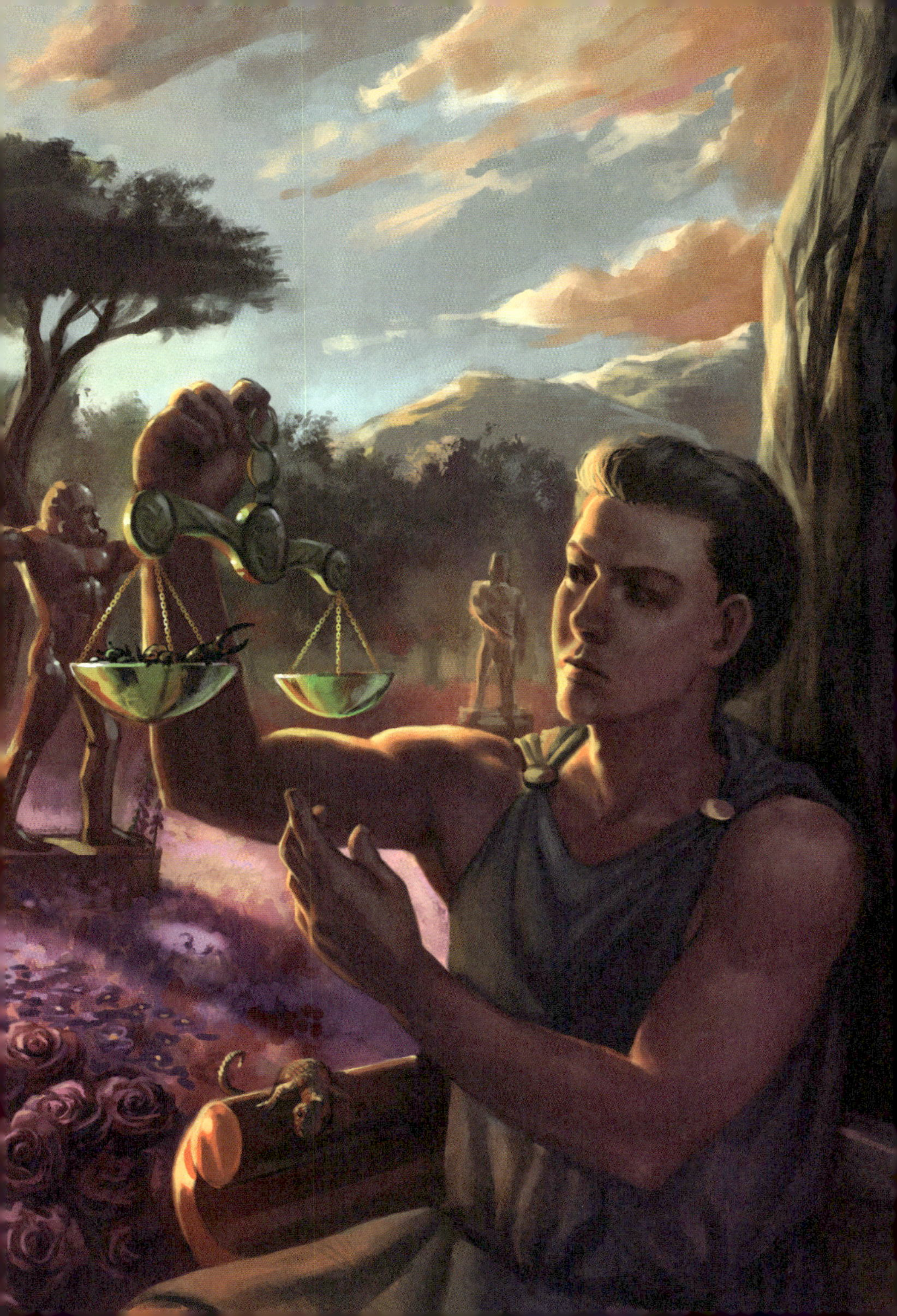

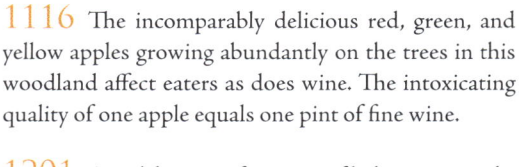

1116 The incomparably delicious red, green, and yellow apples growing abundantly on the trees in this woodland affect eaters as does wine. The intoxicating quality of one apple equals one pint of fine wine.

1201 An 18' diameter fairy ring of light green mushrooms with lilac caps grows on a greensward. In its center lie a suit of leather armor, a cloak, a spear, a dagger, a set of clothing, a canteen, and a backpack holding spoiled rations. Anyone stepping into the center of the fairy ring must make a saving throw or his body (sans possessions) will turn into a swirling green and lilac gas. When the wind blows the gas out of the fairy ring, the person's now-naked body will return to normal. Anytime that such a victim tries to re-enter the fairy ring, he will again turn to gas with no saving throw.

1202 An ancient marble font (15' diameter) amongst aspen holds slightly dirty water. In the center of its 18" deep water is the illusion of a stone coffer roughly 1' square. Anything touching the illusion will pass through but not dispel it. Only while the waters are roughly roiled will the illusion vanish. Anyone stepping into the font will be teleported (no saving throw) to the identical font in hex 0607. Those teleported will be unaware of it. Rather, it will seem that their surroundings outside the font shimmer and change.

1203 Four bipeds (ARMOR: as chain + shield, HD 1, HP 8 each, MOVE 120', 1d4/bite, 1d2/two claws) stand 3' tall and look like humanoid versions of an Asian elephant, a Bengal tiger, an Indian rhinoceros, and a water buffalo (respectively). Only spells of 8th or higher level can affect them. Their tails are 4' long Indian cobras, the venomous bites of which necessitate a saving throw.

1204 Wildflowers chatter animatedly to each other in feminine voices: "How lovely you look today!" "Your color is so much better than yesterday," "A little rain

HEX DESCRIPTIONS

will do wonders for your complexion," etc. They ignore men unless walked through: "How inconsiderate!," "The brutes!," etc. If plucked or chopped, the flowers all fall silent.

1205 To the left of a dark cave opening 5' in diameter stands a gray statue of a gowned woman hiding her face, weeping. The cave stretches 30' back before it ends at a seemingly bottomless pit 9' in diameter. Anyone who enters the cave and peers into the pit will have a −3 on his next saving throw against something that will kill the character if he fails his save.

1206 This creature (ARMOR: as plate + shield, HD 7, HP 26, MOVE 40', 1d8/four claws) is a giant (8' diameter) crab with only four legs, but with four pincers. This beast will attack spellcasters (magic-users before clerics) first, and then it will attack the foe with the fewest remaining hit points. It will infect with a parasite any foe left alone and unconscious with it. The parasite will, over the course of 16 weeks, gradually destroy the mind of the infected victim and transform him into another identical crab monster (but roll 7d8 for hit points). The monster can hear things within 50' even through interposing barriers such as walls, floors, or ceilings. All those coming within 20' of the creature must make a saving throw or come under the control of the creature (a new saving throw is allowed at the end of each round). Since the creature is not intelligent, for the most part this control will manifest either as defending the creature from harm (including attacking fellow party members to defend it), or presenting himself as a defenseless meal for the creature. The crab's claws are all poisonous. Each time a target is stuck by one, he must make a saving throw or take 10 additional points of damage (save for half). The giant crab has a 3 in 6 chance to surprise.

1206

ISLE OF THE UNKNOWN

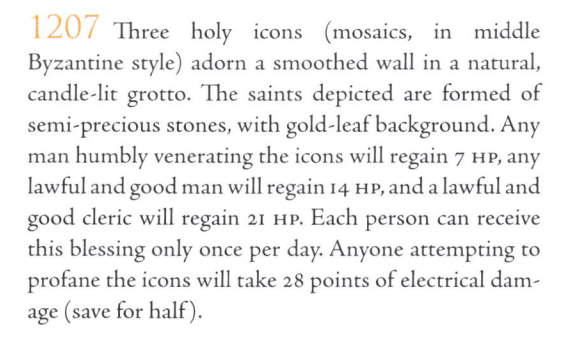

1207 Three holy icons (mosaics, in middle Byzantine style) adorn a smoothed wall in a natural, candle-lit grotto. The saints depicted are formed of semi-precious stones, with gold-leaf background. Any man humbly venerating the icons will regain 7 HP, any lawful and good man will regain 14 HP, and a lawful and good cleric will regain 21 HP. Each person can receive this blessing only once per day. Anyone attempting to profane the icons will take 28 points of electrical damage (save for half).

1208 A four-legged pigeon (ARMOR: none, HD 11, HP 45, MOVE 150' [walk and fly], 3d6+2/claw) is the size of an apatosaurus, and in combat a display of feathers rises behind the creature's head. It can be surprised only 1 in 6, and it only needs to roll 2 or more to save against any magical effect. If it rolls a 20 to hit score (or 4 higher than needed), its claw does an additional 1d8 points of damage. At will the giant pigeon can shape-shift into a giant yellow spider. In this form it can, once per turn, spin a web up to 55 square feet in size. Anyone coming in contact with the web must make a saving throw or be ensnared until cut out by someone.

1209 In the midst of a 100' diameter circle of strangely-colored nature (bright orange stones, purple and yellow grass, red foliage, etc.) stands a life-sized statue of a nude woman made of an unknown, sky blue stone. She holds a rainbow-colored harp. Anyone plucking the strings will notice that random objects (including himself) within 50' turn other colors for nearly a minute before returning to their previous color. During the daylight hours of the first moon of spring and the first moon of autumn, the statue animates and plays her harp, which allows her to turn anything within 50' to whatever color of the rainbow that her whim desires. The color change is permanent unless more than 50' separates the harp from the changed object, in which case the new color fades away after 2d5 moons. If at-

HEX DESCRIPTIONS

tacked, the statue (ARMOR: as plate + shield, HD 11, HP 50, MOVE 40', 1d12/discord) attacks by plucking ear-shattering, discordant notes upon her harp.

1210 A marble statue of a beardless man is covered with dozens of eyes. Any magic-user who touches one of the statue's eyes while closing his own will be able to see any one desired location for up to 15 minutes. This may be done once per week. Any fighter who touches one of the statue's eyes will cause the statue to animate (ARMOR: as plate + shield, HD 10, HP 45, MOVE 40', 2d8/fist) and attack. Nothing will happen if other character types touch the statue.

1211 The children of this town (population 1,600) delight in befriending the kind and holy gardener over the bridge seven miles south (hex 1212).

1212 A 3rd-level cleric (ARMOR: plate + shield, HD 3, HP 10, MOVE 60') spends his days peacefully tending his vegetable and flower gardens. He is immune to any ill effects of the weather. This gentle man is a friend of all beasts, and can speak with them. Though typically dressed only in a simple tunic, if attacked he will miraculously appear in his armor and white-crossed red surcoat, armed with a long sword. He will also call to his defense two cinnamon bears (ARMOR: none, HD 4, HP 20, 17, MOVE 120', 1d8/bite, 1d4/two claws).

1213 Five bipedal aardvarks (ARMOR: as chain, HD 10, HP 45, 41, 39, 48, 47, MOVE 120', 1d6/bite, 1d6/bash, 1d3/tail) are 3' tall and have 4 arms. They can be surprised only 1 in 6, and they take half damage from crushing attacks. They can, at will, cast a *Light* spell and become liquid (in which form they can neither make nor be hurt by mêlée attacks). The aardvark-men are also clairaudient. Worst of all, 24 hours after being wounded by them, a character has a chance (equal to the percentage of original total HP that the monsters

1213

55

inflicted in damage) of transforming into an aardvark-man in 2d20 days. Any such unfortunate will return to join the aardvark-men.

1214 A 280 lb. earwig (ARMOR: as chain, HD 4, HP 16, MOVE 150' [walk and fly], 2d8/forceps) attacks with the multiply razor-edged forceps on its hind quarters. Its eyes are mounted on 2' long eye stalks, ensuring that it is surprised only 1 in 6. This insect can crawl upon walls and ceilings.

1215 A huge butterfly (ARMOR: as chain + shield, HD 6, HP 24, MOVE 150' [fly], 60' [walk], 1d8+1/two claws) has a 12' wingspan. Its body is continuously on fire. Those who come in contact with its body take damage as if splashed by burning oil (in addition to damage from its claws, if applicable). The butterfly can crawl upon walls and ceilings as easily as upon the ground. In combat, it emits a cloud of gas with a 45' radius that causes all within to lose 1 point of dexterity. Lost points of dexterity return at the rate of 1/hour.

1216 A cave bear (ARMOR: as chain + shield, HD 6, HP 31, MOVE 120', 1d8/hug) usually walks upon its hind legs. Its body is covered with open sores that ooze foul pus. Anyone coming in contact with the pus must make a saving throw or run away in abject terror for 1d4 turns. The bear cannot be surprised, and when it hits an opponent, it hugs him and automatically does 1d8 damage each round.

1301 A statue of colorless crystal depicts a young man. Anyone who touches the statue will find a change come over him when he next enters combat: If he makes a saving throw, he becomes invisible for the duration of the combat. If he misses his saving throw, he will turn into an invisible gas for the duration of the combat.

HEX DESCRIPTIONS

1301

1215

57

ISLE OF THE UNKNOWN

1302 Honeysuckle and geraniums bloom year-round in a woodland of hawthorn trees and holly plants. The odor of peppermint suffuses the air. Uncut diamonds and amethysts litter the ground like pebbles. In this idyllic setting dwells a 6th-level magic-user (ARMOR: as chain, HD 6, HP 23, MOVE 90', 1d6/short sword) dressed in a fiery red tunic, with iron sword and armor. He keeps a herd of 101 sheep with (literal!) golden fleeces. If attacked, the magic-user will call upon the 19 rams (ARMOR: as chain, HD 3, HP 11, 7, 11, 17, 14, 16, 14, 14, 20, 9, 16, 19, 15, 12, 13, 11, 19, 12, 14, MOVE 120', 1d4/ram) of his herd who will fight to the death in his defense. Any gems taken from the woods without the magic-user's leave will turn to common pebbles, and golden fleece will turn to cotton. If the magic-user is slain, the enchantment of the woodland will vanish, leaving nothing of value other than the magic-user's armor and short sword.

1303 A giant eagle (ARMOR: as leather + shield, HD 11, HP 46, MOVE 40' [crawl], 100' [fly], 1d8+1/claw) with a 14' wingspan has four legs and can use them to crawl upon walls and ceilings as easily as it can walk on land. Though it has fearsome horns upon its head, it does not use them in combat. This monster will attack any humans in an attempt to reproduce itself. It attacks with such ferocity that it has a +4 bonus to hit. This vindictive creature will aim its attacks at whoever did the most damage to it in the most recent round of attacks. If the beast manages to knock a human unconscious, it will lay an egg inside of him (though only after combat is over). Six weeks later a young monster of the same characteristics as this miscreation will rip out of the victim's belly, killing him instantly. As it is only a baby, it will have but 11 hit points. Roll 11d8 to determine how many HP it will have when full-grown. It will gain 1 HP each week after it is born, up to the number rolled on 11d8. The creature can generate a 10' radius sphere of darkness around itself. It can see in this

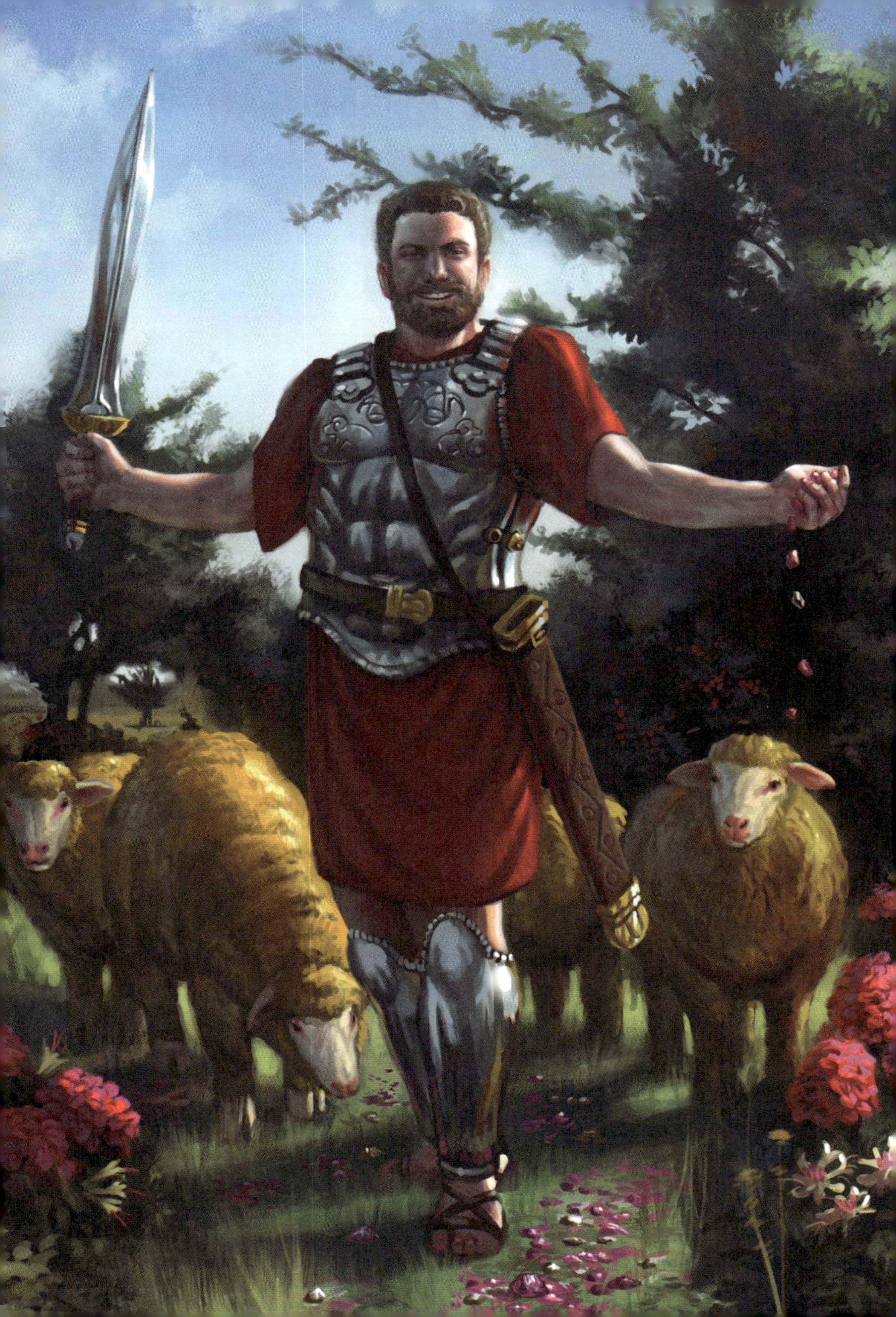

ISLE OF THE UNKNOWN

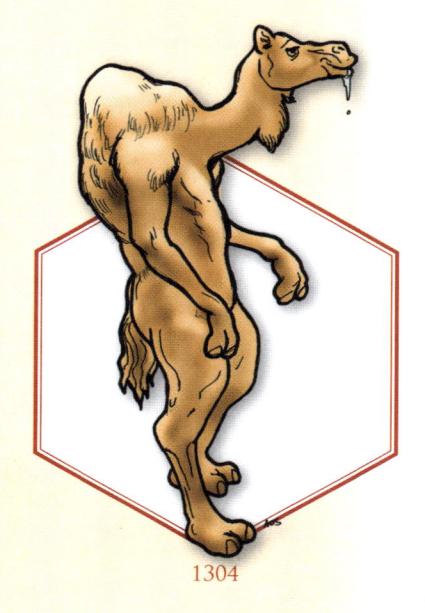

darkness. When entering mêlée, this monster (whether flying or running) will charge, thus doing 2d8+2 points of damage with that attack. Instead of attacking with its claws, the monster can spit a stream of poison up to 30'. The victim must make a saving throw or take 20 points of damage (save for half).

1304 A 6' tall bipedal camel (ARMOR: as chain + shield, HD 4, HP 8, MOVE 120' [jumping], 1d6/freezing spit) attacks by spitting its freezing saliva up to 50'. The creature can turn into a shadow, thereby becoming invisible outside of direct sunlight. In this form it surprises on a 5 in 6, but as a shade it cannot attack nor be attacked by non-magical means.

1305 A 7' tall rat-man (ARMOR: as chain + shield, HD 4, HP 11, MOVE 120' [walk], 1d8+1/claw) exudes such a powerful coconut smell that it can surprise only 1 in 6.

1306 The Loremaster is a hoary 5th-level magic-user (ARMOR: none, HD 5, HP 15, MOVE 90') with a long gray beard. He dwells alone in a small stone tower overlooking the mountain valley. He possesses little besides his voluminous library of books and scrolls. The Loremaster has encyclopedic knowledge of the island- its flora and fauna, history, geography, etc. When his writings fail him, he can often rely upon his magical brazier, the smoke of which will reveal to the Loremaster (alone) much lost lore of the isle. Since treasure means little to him, he usually requires his suppliants to acquire and bring to him forgotten scrolls hidden in the ancient ruins found on the island.

1307 In a damp, shady spot of the forest swells a 3' tall white mushroom with an orange-red cap dotted with white warts. Similar mushrooms only a few inches high surround it. The large mushroom has intelligence

Hex Descriptions

at least equal to a man's, and it can speak the common language of the isle.

1308　In a clearing amidst the forest stand 37 statues of gray stone. All but one depict persons grimacing in pain and/or fear. The lone exception is of a grim, muscular man in a loincloth holding a large hammer. When anyone enters the clearing, this statue becomes conscious and waits for his best opportunity to attack (thus allowing the statue to surprise 95 % of the time). If the animated statue (ARMOR: as plate + shield, HD 11, HP 50, MOVE 40', 4d12/hammer) reduces an opponent to 0 or fewer HP, the victim turns to stone.

1309　A 300 lb. scorpion-man (ARMOR: as chain, HD 4, HP 20, MOVE 120' [walk], 40' [tunneling], 1d6/two claws, 1d8/tail) walks upon two legs and uses its other six legs for manipulation. It is continually drenched in its own pale greenish blood. This monster can easily crawl upon walls and ceilings.

1310　In the shadows of dark oak trees swell patches of fungi with black caps and sickly white stems. The odor exhaling from the fungus makes people see beneath the deceptive loveliness of life and nature (save avoids). Everything seems old and funereal. Trees appear ancient and gnarled. Flowers seem like fungus, while trees and animals vanish from sight. Men seem to be animate, naked skeletons that merely clack their teeth when they attempt speech. This macabre vision lasts 3d8 hours.

1311　Standing in deep forest, a statue of moss- and mica-covered rock depicts a barbarian clothed in a bear's skin, wielding a gnarled club. If any living flora is deliberately harmed within 200 yards of this statue, it will animate (ARMOR: as plate + shield, HD 11, HP 50, MOVE 90', 3d12/club) and fiercely attack.

1309

ISLE OF THE UNKNOWN

1312   A 6′ tall statue of a bald man is made of translucent crystal. The upper fourth is red, the next fourth is colorless, the next fourth is blue, and the bottom fourth is amber-colored. The first person in spring to touch the blue part will be able to turn himself into a medium-sized water elemental for 15 minutes one time that spring. The first person in summer to touch the red part will be able to turn himself into a medium-sized fire elemental for 15 minutes one time that summer. The first person in fall to touch the amber part will be able to turn himself into a medium-sized earth elemental for 15 minutes one time that fall. The first person in winter to touch the colorless part will be able to turn himself into a medium-sized air elemental for 15 minutes one time that winter. Nothing will happen to other men touching the appropriate part of the statue in the correct season. If a person touches the wrong part in the wrong season, he will take 2d10 points of elemental damage (fire for red, air for colorless, water for blue, and earth for amber), with a saving throw indicating half damage.

1313   A pair of similar statues is hewn from a midnight blue rock and stands 20′ high. On nights of the new moon they will animate (ARMOR: as plate + shield, HD 12, HP 54, MOVE 90′, 4d6/fist) and attack any human they see. They are immune to normal weapons, though silver weapons are effective. When animated they radiate a power of blindness. Those within 50′ of them must make a saving throw at the beginning of each round or be blinded for that round.

1314   Atop a mountain above tree line stands a sandstone statue of a bearded man 6′ tall, holding a javelin in its right hand. Hundreds of hawks reside in a 100 yard radius of the statue. If anyone seeks to harm the statue or any of the hawks, the statue will animate (ARMOR: as plate + shield, HD 13, HP MOVE 40′, 3d6/javelin). When the statue is in combat, the hawks will attack en masse,

HEX DESCRIPTIONS

automatically doing 4 points of damage each round and causing their victims to attack at −2.

1315 A 7' tall parrot (ARMOR: as leather, HD 8, HP 35, MOVE 240' [fly], 120' [walk], 1d10/beak) not only has predominantly red plumage, but is actually on fire. Anyone coming into physical contact with the monster will take damage as if splashed by burning oil.

1316 This monster (ARMOR: as leather, HD 9, HP 48, MOVE 40', 1d8/slam) has an 8' tall body shaped like a four-sided pyramid surmounted by an eagle's head and (flightless) wings. Four avian legs support the body. The thing is completely covered with long, thick fur of a very light brown color with yellow at the five corners of the pyramid. This monster feeds on fear, and will therefore attack any who fear it. Conversely, it will leave those alone who do not fear it. It prefers to attack opponents who wear the least amount of armor. Failing that, it will attack whoever is closest. It attacks by bashing its body against its victims. The creature can be damaged only by silver weapons. Beginning on the round after it first suffers damage, this monster will regenerate 2 HP/round. Even after being reduced to 0 (or fewer) hit points, it will regenerate. Only damage caused by fire will not regenerate.

1401 A 3' diameter natural shaft leads 20' down to a 30' long passage that ends in a cavern roughly 30' in diameter with a 12' high ceiling. Littering the floor are several old, broken human skeletons, along with an ancient cup of harlequin opal (worth 5,000 g.p.). Near the far wall stands a statue of pale green limestone, in the shape of a man. Bloodstains blotch the statue and the ground near it. If anyone attempts to leave the cavern without spilling human blood (even a drop will do) on the statue or on the ground within 6' of the statue, it will animate (ARMOR: as plate + shield, HD 11, HP 50, MOVE 40', 3d6/two fists) and attack.

1316

ISLE OF THE UNKNOWN

1402 A man-sized statue is plated with gold and holds a silver long sword in each hand. Six long swords, five short swords, three broad swords, and a two-handed sword are piled at its feet. Anyone who approaches the statue within 10' without leaving a sword at the statue's feet will cause the statue to animate (ARMOR: as plate + shield, HD 10, HP 45, MOVE 90', 1d12/two swords) and attack with both its swords each round. If an attacked person drops his sword and flees, the statue will not pursue.

1403 A pale gray stone statue will change form and countenance each time the player characters move at least 1 mile away from it. It might appear as a child, an old man, a warrior, a nude maiden, a witch, a king, etc. There is a 2% chance of the statue instead appearing as a tunic-clad man of medium build with no face.

1404 A 200 lb. monster (ARMOR: as leather +shield, HD 4, HP 20, MOVE 130' [walk and swim], 1d8/bite) has the body, eyes, and front and hind legs of a grasshopper, while its head and midmost legs are those of a duck. Small oak-like branches with green leaves grow from its body. This abomination can walk upon walls and ceilings. No human or mundane animal can come within 10' of the beast. If its to hit roll is a 20 (or 4 or more needed to hit), then its bite causes 3d8 points of damage.

1405 A cave holds a pool about 8' in diameter and 2' to 3' deep. Therein lives a blue-green woman of heartbreaking beauty and with eyes of fathomless sorrow. Her life is tied to the pool, which is the last, pitiful remnant of a forgotten sea. Unimaginably old, the woman weeps to remember her lost world, which will wholly perish when the pool finally dwindles to nothing.

1406 This monster (ARMOR: as leather, HD 5, HP 28, MOVE 30' [slither], 90' [fly], 1d12/bite) is a 16' long leg-

Hex Descriptions

less lizard with the wings of a bat. While the creature will attack most humans out of unreasoning hatred, any magically affected character (cursed, polymorphed, etc.) will not be attacked by the creature except in self-defense. In combat it prefers to attack the most heavily armored foe. This creature is hard to surprise (1 in 6 chance).

1407 A thorn bush bears large, sensuous, velvety-black roses. Their seductive fragrance causes 1d8 points of damage per round to anyone within 5'. Each round beginning with the second, anyone inhaling the lethal perfumes must make a saving throw to tear himself away from the promised, blissful death.

1408 A 160 lb. fly (ARMOR: as shield, HD 7, HP 26, MOVE 240' [fly], 100' [walk], 1d6+1/two claws) has a 10' long, serpentine-shaped body with a rubbery consistency. Any attack that does less than half its possible damage bounces off without harm. Missile weapons so bouncing have a 10 % chance of striking a random combatant. It can crawl upon walls and ceilings as easily as upon floors. The fly gets a +1 to initiative, and a +4 to all its saving throws. If both of its claws hit the same target in the same round, they do maximum damage. The monster can become incorporeal at will, in which state it can neither attack nor attacked by physical means. Strangely enough, it can turn itself into a pale orange snapper fish about 3' long. It typically does this when it needs to flee (assuming a body of water is available).

1409 This bizarre entity (ARMOR: none, HD 6, HP 28, MOVE 60' [walk], 80' [fly]) is an incorporeal, four-legged crane that stands 150' tall. It is covered with (corporeal) slime, pus, and foul goop streaming from open sores on its incorporeal body. This monster's incorporeal body makes it unable to physically attack. It feeds on fear, and will not attack those who feel no fear in its presence. Those who do feel fear, however, the

1408

1409

1409

creature will attempt to target using its special abilities. It prefers to attack spellcasters (magic-users before clerics). If no spellcasters are present and afraid, then its target will be determined randomly each round. The creature is able to make a 6" thick barrier of solid ice of 150 square feet, in any shape desired. The creature may create such a barrier once per turn. Anyone coming into contact with the ooze streaming from the monster's body must make a saving throw or come under the control of the creature for 1d4 rounds. Since the creature is not intelligent, for the most part the creature will only command those under its control to defend it from harm (including forcing controlled characters to attack allies that threaten it) or to commit suicide. Only magical attacks (and attacks with silver weapons) affect it, and it can not physically attack others.

1410

A 20' tall statue of iron depicts a smith raising his hammer above an anvil with lettering that reads, "TOUCH NOT THE TREASURE". An illusory horde of wrought gold and coins surrounds the anvil. If the illusion is touched, it vanishes and the statue animates (ARMOR: as plate + shield, HD 11, HP 50, MOVE 40', 5d8/hammer) and attacks with its now red-hot hammer. The illusion will return one hour after vanishing.

1411

A 7' tall red-copper statue of a long-haired nude woman grasps a curved knife's hilt in one hand and its tip in the other. If anyone seeks vengeance against a human enemy, he can touch his weapons (or hands if a magic-user) to the statue's knife while thinking of his enemy. For the next three months, any of his attacks against his enemy will be at +3 to hit and damage. His spells will also be unusually effective against his enemy (−3 penalty to saving throws). If the statue is damaged, it will attack (ARMOR: as plate + shield, HD 13, HP 59, MOVE 60', 2d12/knife).

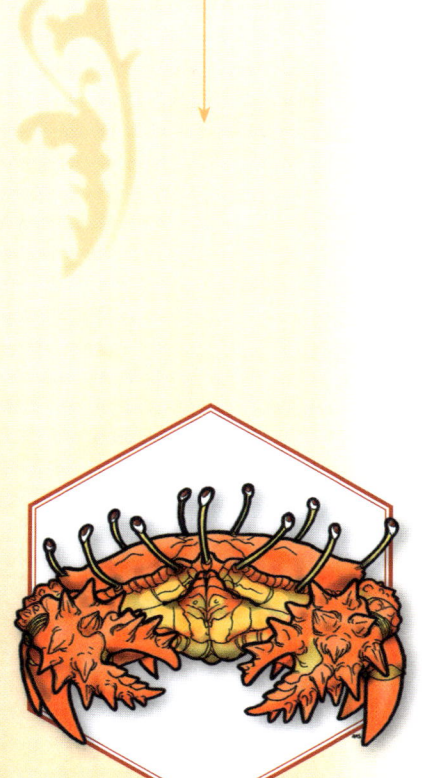

1412

Hex Descriptions

1412 A 250 lb. crab (ARMOR: as plate, HD 10, HP 60, MOVE 120', 2d6/two claws) has spike-covered claws and 11 eyestalks, which give it only a 1 in 12 chance of being surprised. It is also immune to mind-affecting magic. If the crab charges into mêlée, its initial claw attacks each do 4d6 points of damage. Three of its eyestalks have a magical attack (save avoids) with a range of 60', and any one of these attacks can be made once per round: A) *Charm Person* spell; B) −2 to saves, to-hit rolls, and armor for 1d4 turns; C) all food and drink carried become spoiled.

1413 Five 4' tall humanoid bats (ARMOR: none, HD 13, HP 51, 67, 55, 60, 64, MOVE 90' [walk], 120' [fly], 1d6/bite, 1d6/stinger) have long tails tipped with stingers. A hit by a stinger makes a random limb useless for 4d4 days (save avoids). They are immune to mind-affecting magic, fire, and normal weapons. The fur of a bat-man shifts color according to his surroundings, giving it a +2 chance to surprise. Their eyes can glow as bright as a lantern.

1414 A prairie is continuously about 95° Fahrenheit because of the unearthly sunflowers growing there. Some say that the flowers originally grew on the sun itself. They are too hot to touch and never die as long as they remain in the prairie. At night they shed a yellow glow equal to moonlight. If picked, over the course of a week the flowers gradually lose their heat and luminescence.

1415 A 7' tall humanoid trout (ARMOR: as chain, HD 7, HP 41, MOVE 120' [walk, swim, and fly], 1d8/two bashes) is amphibious and has a rubbery body. Any attack that does less than half its possible damage bounces off without harm. Missile weapons so bouncing have a 10% chance of striking a random combatant. This monster regenerates 2 HP/round, even after being reduced to fewer than 0 HP. Only damage done by bronze weapons does not regenerate. In lieu of mêlée attacks, the trout-man can generate a 110' long cone (with a 45° arc) of disintegration. Those caught within the cone must make a saving throw or be vaporized.

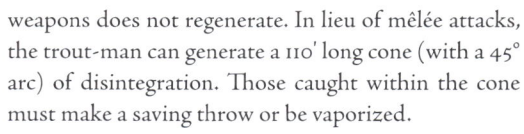

1416 This man-sized cockroach (ARMOR: as chain, HD 2, HP 10, MOVE 120', 1d4/four claws) walks upon its two back limbs as easily upon walls and ceilings as upon the ground. Its wings allow it to glide (but not actually fly) from high elevations to lower surfaces. Nearly half of this monster's body is covered with short, black hair.

1503 A 19' tall bipedal fox (ARMOR: none, HD 5, HP 28, MOVE 130', 2d8/bite) slithers upon the ground rather than walks. Its red fur is mottled with violet patches. Though unintelligent, it can imitate human speech like a parrot. During combat, it will say in a high-pitched, feminine voice, "Get out of here! My God!" followed by a harrowing scream.

1504 A 7' tall humanoid wolf (ARMOR: as chain + shield, HD 2, HP 13, MOVE 130', 1d12/bite) has black fur and a maroon crab shell upon its back. The shell has a vertical purple stripe.

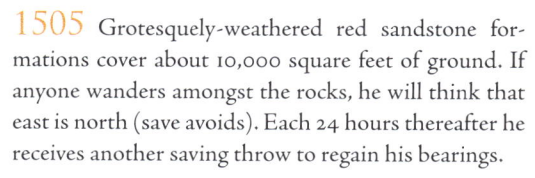

1505 Grotesquely-weathered red sandstone formations cover about 10,000 square feet of ground. If anyone wanders amongst the rocks, he will think that east is north (save avoids). Each 24 hours thereafter he receives another saving throw to regain his bearings.

1506 A 5' tall bipedal skunk (ARMOR: as leather, HD 1, HP 7, MOVE 120' [fly only], 1d8/bash) has bat-like wings with a 6' wingspan. It strikes opponents with these wings. If this monster is slain, 3 weeks later its slayer will have been tracked-down by the thing that spawned it. This beast (ARMOR: as leather, HD 4, HP

Hex Descriptions

18, move 150' [fly only], 2d8/bash) looks like a 10' tall version of its progeny.

1507 Within a labyrinthine cavern lurks a diabolic high priest, a 9th-level cleric (armor: plate, hd 9, hp 43, move 60') in black armor and armed with a scimitar and a curved dagger. The sooty blackness impedes not the priest, as he can see even in utter darkness as though it were clear daylight. When he so wills, all men within 60' fall to the ground with incapacitating pain. (A saving throw is allowed at the beginning of each round to be unaffected that round.) He can also extinguish all non-magical light (such as torches and lanterns) within 60' without fail. Only one power can be used each round. Twelve 0-level men-at-arms (armor: leather, hd 1d6, hp 4, 6, 4, 6, 4, 4, 6, 4, 4, 5, 6, 5 move 120') with scimitars serve the cleric.

1508 A 5' diameter amoeba (armor: none, hd 4, hp 19, move 120', 1d6/caustic touch) is red with blue stripes. It can project a 4' long prehensile "tongue" that can lift up to 60 pounds.

1504

1508

1506

ISLE OF THE UNKNOWN

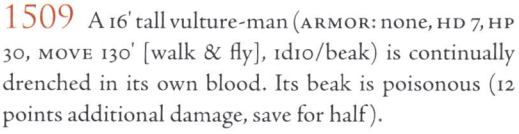

1509 A 16' tall vulture-man (ARMOR: none, HD 7, HP 30, MOVE 130' [walk & fly], 1d10/beak) is continually drenched in its own blood. Its beak is poisonous (12 points additional damage, save for half).

1510 This monster (ARMOR: as leather, HD 12, HP 51, MOVE 50', 1d10+1/claw) is a huge, 20' long pig with sharp claws. This beast prefers to attack opponents with the heaviest armor. Any foe left alone and unconscious will be infected by the monster with a parasite, which will slowly (over the course of 17 weeks) destroy the mind of the infected and transform it into another giant pig monster. If the creature's attack roll hits by 4 or more higher than needed, or is a natural 20, the creature does an additional 1d6 damage in addition to the normal damage. The creature can change its colors to match its background (thus surprising 4 in 6). The creature is effectively invisible if it can get 50' away from the nearest foe. The venom in the pig's claws does an additional 20 points of damage (save for half). This monster is surprised only 1 in 6.

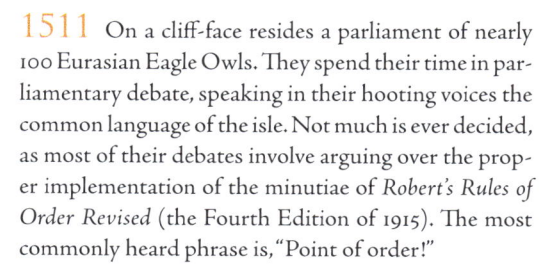

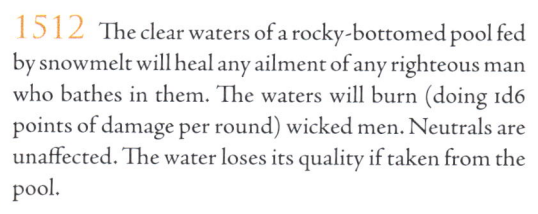

1511 On a cliff-face resides a parliament of nearly 100 Eurasian Eagle Owls. They spend their time in parliamentary debate, speaking in their hooting voices the common language of the isle. Not much is ever decided, as most of their debates involve arguing over the proper implementation of the minutiae of *Robert's Rules of Order Revised* (the Fourth Edition of 1915). The most commonly heard phrase is, "Point of order!"

1512 The clear waters of a rocky-bottomed pool fed by snowmelt will heal any ailment of any righteous man who bathes in them. The waters will burn (doing 1d6 points of damage per round) wicked men. Neutrals are unaffected. The water loses its quality if taken from the pool.

HEX DESCRIPTIONS

1513 Thick fog perpetually shrouds this forest of fir trees. No animal comes here, nor does the wind blow through the trees. An eerie stillness reigns.

1514 A 6' tall alligator-man (ARMOR: as leather + shield, HD 3, HP 17, MOVE 120' [walk and swim], 1d8/bite) takes no damage from blunt weapons. The poison in its bite does an additional 10 points of damage (save at +2 for half). The monster can shapeshift at will into a giant Venus Flytrap (ARMOR: none, HD 3, HP 17, MOVE none, 1d10/bite).

1515 A statue of black stone represents a grim and evil-visaged man. Anyone who sees the statue will experience exhausting nightmares if he sleeps within 5 miles of the statue. Such an unfortunate will not heal any hit points or be able to regain spells that day.

1516 A black stone statue oozes blood over most of its surface. The statue will animate (ARMOR: as plate + shield, HD 12, HP 54, MOVE 30', 2d12/flaming touch), bursting into black flame, and attack anyone who touches the blood.

1601 A scholarly sect has rebuilt the ruins of an ancient building. Within reside exactly 50 hierophantic scholars who follow the intellectual and esoteric traditions of the Platonist philosopher, Proclus. They will gladly illuminate visitors with their wisdom, though they keep secret their antediluvian lore of the mysteries of the star, Sirius. These academicians venerate (but do not accord divine worship to) a statue of a hideously ugly amalgamation of a dolphin and a man.

1602 A clawed 17' tall giraffe (ARMOR: as plate, HD 3, HP 18, MOVE 150', 2d6+2/claw) looks as though it is made of gray granite. Rocks and minerals simply do not exist for this creature. It effortlessly passes through them.

1514

1602

ISLE OF THE UNKNOWN

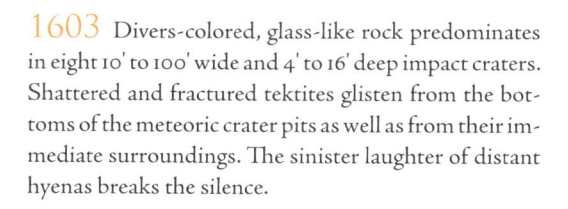

1603 Divers-colored, glass-like rock predominates in eight 10' to 100' wide and 4' to 16' deep impact craters. Shattered and fractured tektites glisten from the bottoms of the meteoric crater pits as well as from their immediate surroundings. The sinister laughter of distant hyenas breaks the silence.

1604 A 9th-level cleric (ARMOR: plate + shield, HD 9, HP 33, MOVE 60') in a red surcoat with a white cross rides southeast to take ship upon a holy pilgrimage. He bears a mace and a dagger. In battle the cleric can make a fiery sun-like sphere (3' diameter) appear before his foes. The sphere strobes all the colors of the rainbow and rushes hither and yon with a low roaring sound. Each foe must make a saving throw each round or fall to the ground in fear and awe, unable to do aught for the rest of the combat (unless attacked, in which case counter-attack is possible). During this miracle, the fragrance of roses fills the air, and afterwards rose petals the color of martyr's blood float to the ground.

1605 A waterfall about 6' high gently plashes in a secluded bower. Anyone spending more than 5 minutes of silence in the bower will seem to hear the waters whispering unceasingly, "Where the winds? Where the winds?"

1606 A statue of dark gray stone depicts a young man with eagle's wings. The statue will animate (ARMOR: as plate + shield, HD 12, HP 54, MOVE 90' [fly], 60' [walk], 3d6/choke) and attack everyone present if touched or if approached within 20' for more than 1 minute. With a successful to hit roll, the statue has grabbed his victim by the neck and will automatically do 3d6 points of damage every round thereafter.

1607 Two 5' long lizards (ARMOR: as plate + shield, HD 11, HP 46, 52, MOVE 130', 1d6/bite) emit steam and occasionally jets of boiling water from their bodies. This

1607

HEX DESCRIPTIONS

intense body heat makes them take only half damage from either cold or fire attacks. These monsters are surprised only on a 1 in 6. Their bite is poisonous (16 points additional damage, save at −2 for half), and if the attack roll is a natural 20 (or 4 over what is needed to hit), the bite causes an additional 2d10 points of damage. Once they bite a victim, they do not let go and continue to automatically do 1d6 damage each round. Finally, they can fire a ray from their eyes that drains 1d6 points of wisdom. Lost points of wisdom return 1 per hour.

1608 A centaur-like salamander (ARMOR: as chain + shield, HD 7, HP 23, MOVE 140', 1d12/bite) uses four of its legs for walking and its front two limbs for manipulating objects. It is the size of a moose, and it has noticeably large fangs and a 3' long prehensile tongue. The beast is immune to mental attack, and its bite is poisonous (10 points additional damage, save at +1 for half). Three times per day, it can exude a caustic gas from its skin, forming a 90' diameter cloud centered on itself. Those within the cloud take 7d6 points of damage (save for half damage).

1609 A tarn of blue water will teleport anyone who steps within it to a pool of water in hex 0504. No saving throw applies. If a creature is teleported here from the pool in 0504, he will not be able to magically teleport through the tarn for 28 days.

1610 Above tree line in the snow flourish flowers of the pallid and delicate hues of a lunar rainbow. At night they softly shimmer with a frosty radiance.

1611 An elephant-sized bipedal pig (ARMOR: as leather, HD 10, HP 53, MOVE 130' [slither], 2d6+2/claw) slithers upon its belly rather than walks. Its eyes glow a deep purple, which makes it 1 in 6 less likely to surprise. Crushing attacks do no damage to it. Its claw attack also drains 1d6 points of constitution (which return 1

1608

1611

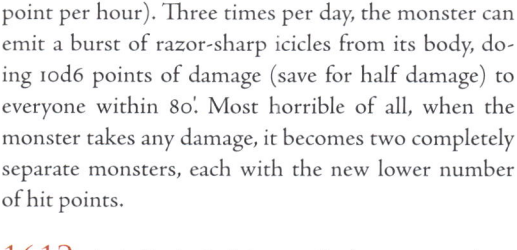

point per hour). Three times per day, the monster can emit a burst of razor-sharp icicles from its body, doing 10d6 points of damage (save for half damage) to everyone within 80'. Most horrible of all, when the monster takes any damage, it becomes two completely separate monsters, each with the new lower number of hit points.

1612 A six-limbed albino gorilla (ARMOR: as chain + shield, HD 7, HP 29, MOVE 120', 1d8+1/grip) moves by slithering its body, using either two limbs or four. It surprises 3 in 6. It attacks with its front left hand, which is covered with short spikes. After successfully gripping an opponent with that hand, it continues to squeeze without letting go, thus automatically doing 1d8+1 points of damage each round thereafter. Any weapon that hits this monster will shatter (though the weapon will do its standard damage).

1613 A bizarre mushroom (ARMOR: none, HD 5, HP 16, MOVE 140' [rolling], 1d8+1/four claws) is 6' in diameter and shaped like a dodecahedron (i.e., the 12-sided Platonic solid). Rending claws on tough, spindly arms grow out of four of its sides. Outside of direct sunlight, this entity can become a living shadow. As such, it is invisible and surprises 5 in 6. In this form it cannot attack or be physically attacked (though spells affect it).

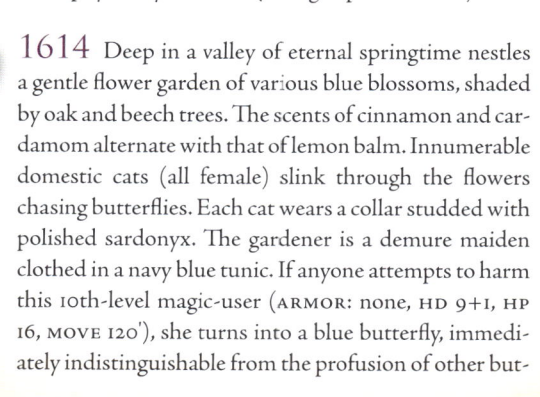

1614 Deep in a valley of eternal springtime nestles a gentle flower garden of various blue blossoms, shaded by oak and beech trees. The scents of cinnamon and cardamom alternate with that of lemon balm. Innumerable domestic cats (all female) slink through the flowers chasing butterflies. Each cat wears a collar studded with polished sardonyx. The gardener is a demure maiden clothed in a navy blue tunic. If anyone attempts to harm this 10th-level magic-user (ARMOR: none, HD 9+1, HP 16, MOVE 120'), she turns into a blue butterfly, immediately indistinguishable from the profusion of other but-

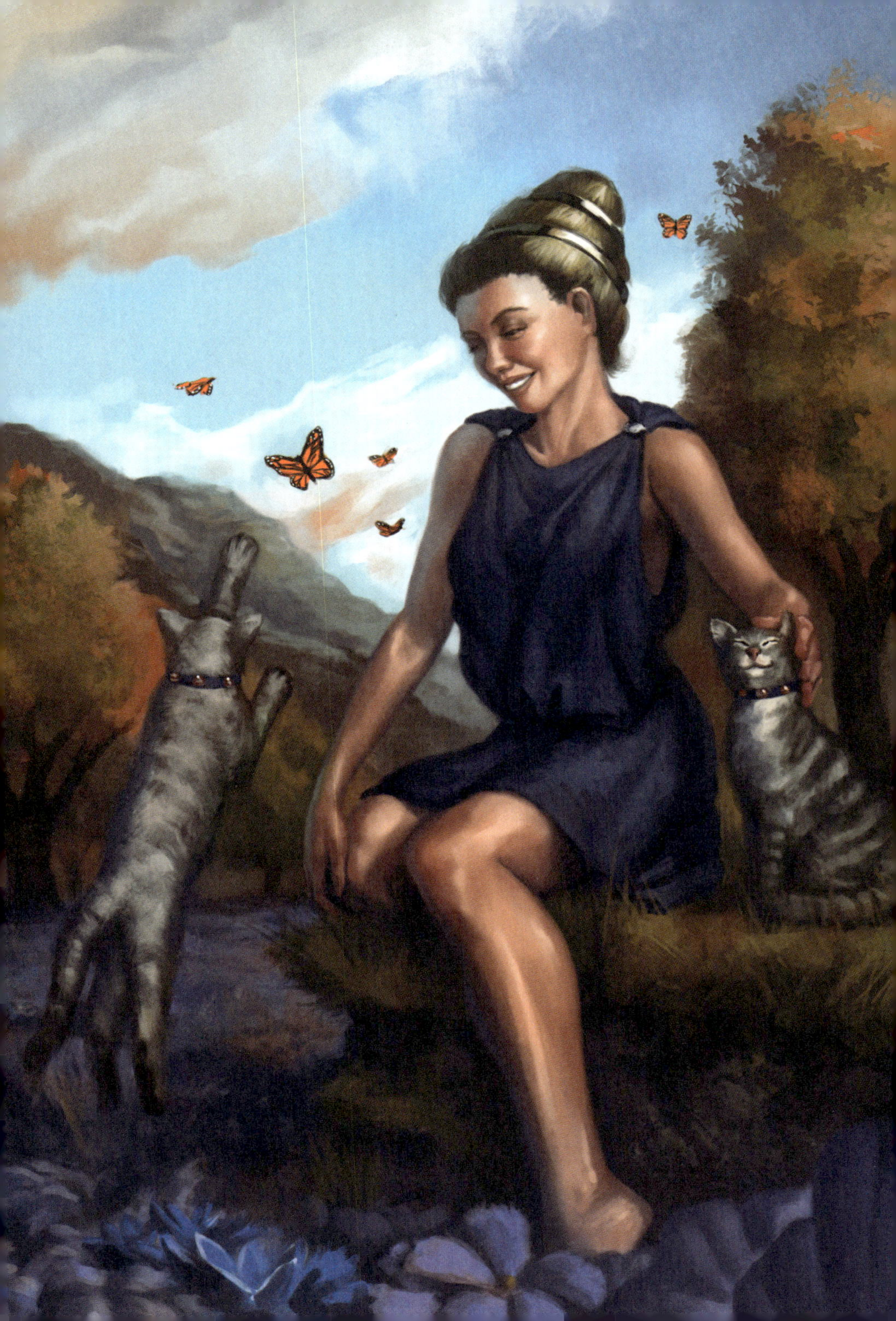

terflies in the garden. If a sardonyx collar is taken out of the garden, it transforms into a *Smilodon* (ARMOR: as leather, HD 8, HP 45, MOVE 180', 3d6/bite, 2d4/two claws) which automatically attacks with surprise.

1615 A gentle and sporadic shower of deep green raindrops falls upon the sward. Where each drop splashes, a lime green frog ½" in diameter jumps up.

1702 A statue is carved from a grayish-white stone, and it represents a long-haired and long-bearded elder king with an imperious demeanor. If the statue is touched in the day, nothing happens. The mind of he who touches the statue in the night will be filled with visions of the terrible grandeur of the pagan kings of ancient days.

1703 A small, stream-fed pool holds slightly luminous orange water. Any magic-user (up to once per day per magic-user) who bathes in the waters will have his full complement of spells restored to his memory.

1704 A flock of 99 pure white sheep grazes peacefully around a 20' tall iron statue of a naked cyclops holding a spear. If anyone worries the sheep or attempts to damage the statue, it radiates a burst of intense cold that causes 3d4 points of damage to those within 15'. If this is not enough to dissuade mischief, the statue will speak an ear-splitting dolorous word (range: long bow, damage 6d10, no saving throw). If anyone dares to continue to molest the sheep or the cyclops, it will animate (ARMOR: as plate + shield, HD 14, HP 63, MOVE 20', 4d12/spear) and pursue for up to 1 mile.

1705 A household of twelve normal humans nestles in a hidden valley of magical flowers. The dwellers here gain nourishment from inhaling the perfumes of the flowers, rather than from eating and drinking. Anyone spending 28 days in the valley will be unable to gain sus-

Hex Descriptions

tenance from anything other than the fragrance of the valley's blossoms (save avoids). If the first saving throw succeeds, each additional 28 days in the valley necessitates another saving throw until one is finally failed.

1706 A statue of brown-green stone depicts a man in a traveling hat and cloak, and he holds a walking stick in his right hand. If anyone grasps the walking stick and utters a direction and a distance (i.e., "50 miles northwest"), he will be so teleported.

1707 Instead of flowing down, a waterfall flows up out of a stream-fed pool to empty into another pool 30' above. The waterfall will sweep anyone touching it into the higher pool.

1708 A giant rat (ARMOR: as leather, HD 8, HP 43, MOVE 130', 1d8/bite, 1d10/two axes, 1d8/spittle) is the size of an African lion. Its forepaws are of bone shaped like great axes, and the beast rears up to attack with them. The giant rat also has caustic spittle, which it can spew up to 20' in lieu of its mêlée attacks.

1709 A statue is made of absolutely colorless and clear crystal, depicting a nondescript man. Its glow of white light is apparent even in full daylight. If the statue is touched, the color of the glow will change according to the toucher's alignment: golden for lawful, blood red for chaotic, and no change for neutral. (If a nine-fold alignment scheme is used, the colors are as follows: golden for LG, emerald for NG, azure for CG, aqua for LN, no change for N, violet for CN, deep purple for LE, dark magenta for NE, and blood red for CE.)

1710 A 24' tall humanoid deer (ARMOR: as leather + shield, HD 12, HP 52, MOVE 140', 2d8/bite) has long gray hair like a woman's. The creature can generate a sphere of darkness (20' radius), and it can also create simple illusions to help it ambush prey.

ISLE OF THE UNKNOWN

1711 A giant piranha (ARMOR: as chain, HD 10, HP 42, MOVE 130′ [swim], 1d8/bite) has a 40′ long, sinuous body that trails ooze. It can see even in utter blackness. It is immune to all mental attacks, it can be struck only by wooden weapons, and it takes only half damage from fire. Once every turn the piranha can stun (save to avoid) all within 90′ for 1d8+1 rounds.

1712 A 9′ tall bipedal fox (ARMOR: as leather, HD 8, HP 43, MOVE 120′, 1d10/bite) is an albino with pink eyes.

1713 A 30′ high mound of granite fragments steadily glows with a hueless light, visible a mile away. It rests in the center of a 2 mile diameter sphere of distorted space. The space within the sphere has a diameter of 200 miles. Thus someone within the sphere who travels 1 mile will appear (to the vision of an outside observer) to travel only about 53′.

1714 A statue of rich purple stone depicts a smiling naked man emptying an amphora upon the ground. Actual red wine continuously pours from the amphora, forming a small pool upon the rocky ground. If a person so much as tastes the wine, he will be thrown into a joyous, drunken ecstasy for the next 24 hours (during which time he can do nothing of a non-festive nature). Afterwards he will find his body 1 year younger. This wine can be efficaciously imbibed once every six months.

1715 An enormous butterfly (ARMOR: as plate + shield, HD 9, HP 43, MOVE 60′ [fly], 30′ [walk], 2d6+2/claws, 1d8/bite) has a 30′ wingspan. Its wings resemble rock, while its body is mechanical. It can crawl upon walls and ceilings as easily as upon the ground.

1801 Lush grass covers this treeless isle. Rough white stone dots the island, and streams of pure water

HEX DESCRIPTIONS

flow from an endlessly gushing natural fountain near its center. A 7' tall Celtic cross of white stone stands near the fountain. Any pious person on this island will heal 3d6 HP each hour, and any other physical harm (blindness, maiming, poison, disease, etc.) will vanish after 1 hour. Neutral persons will experience a sense of peace, but will gain no other benefit. Wicked men, monsters, and noxious beasts will absolutely refuse to set foot upon the island.

1802   A minotaur-like creature (ARMOR: as shield, HD 8, HP 39, MOVE 130', 1d10/two fists) has a 6' long, reticulated neck that makes the beast stand a total of 15' tall. It surprises 11 out of 12, and it takes only half damage from physical attacks. Once every 3 rounds this monster breathes forth a gas that requires everyone within 10' to make two saving throws: the first against poison (20 points damage, save at +1 for half), and the second to avoid paralysis that lasts 1d4 rounds.

1712

1715

79

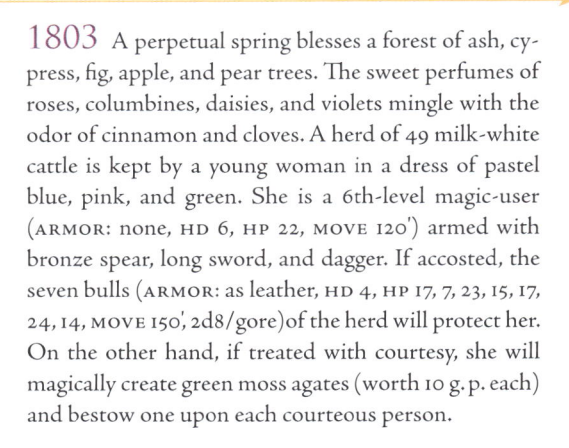

1803 A perpetual spring blesses a forest of ash, cypress, fig, apple, and pear trees. The sweet perfumes of roses, columbines, daisies, and violets mingle with the odor of cinnamon and cloves. A herd of 49 milk-white cattle is kept by a young woman in a dress of pastel blue, pink, and green. She is a 6th-level magic-user (ARMOR: none, HD 6, HP 22, MOVE 120') armed with bronze spear, long sword, and dagger. If accosted, the seven bulls (ARMOR: as leather, HD 4, HP 17, 7, 23, 15, 17, 24, 14, MOVE 150', 2d8/gore) of the herd will protect her. On the other hand, if treated with courtesy, she will magically create green moss agates (worth 10 g.p. each) and bestow one upon each courteous person.

1804 Underneath a stand of ponderosa pine lie scores of pine cones. Close inspection will reveal that the scales of about one-third of these pine cones have a lining of blue-green, silvery-blue, or silver. Touching one of these oddly-colored cones will cause it to float a few inches in the air and spin like a top for 1 minute before gently settling back to the earth.

1805 A man-sized bipedal frog (ARMOR: as plate + shield, HD 6, HP 25, MOVE 120' [fly], 1d8/bite) is a glossy ebony. It can move only by flying, and it cannot be surprised. Once per turn, the monster can spit an adhesive slime covering 30 square feet. Anyone coming into contact with the slime must save or become ensnared in the slime until freed by another. If a human is slain by this beast, within 3d12 hours the unfortunate victim will transform into and rise as an identical creature. A *Remove Curse* spell will return him to human form.

1806 In a hidden valley stand the ruins of an ancient, deserted city. Monolithic statues, 25' high, with Easter Island-like heads, stare towards the temple in the center of the city. Within the temple a dazzling green flame (30' high) rises from a bottomless pit, and an enticingly ecstatic music emanates from the

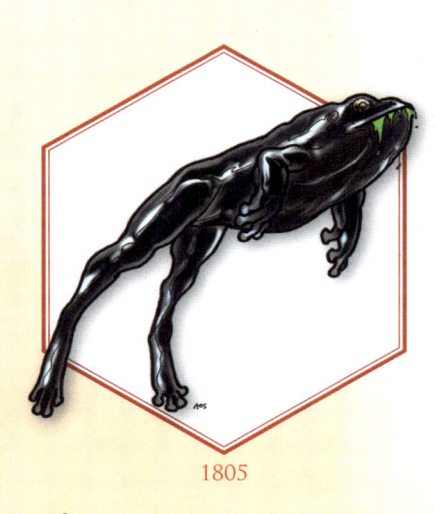

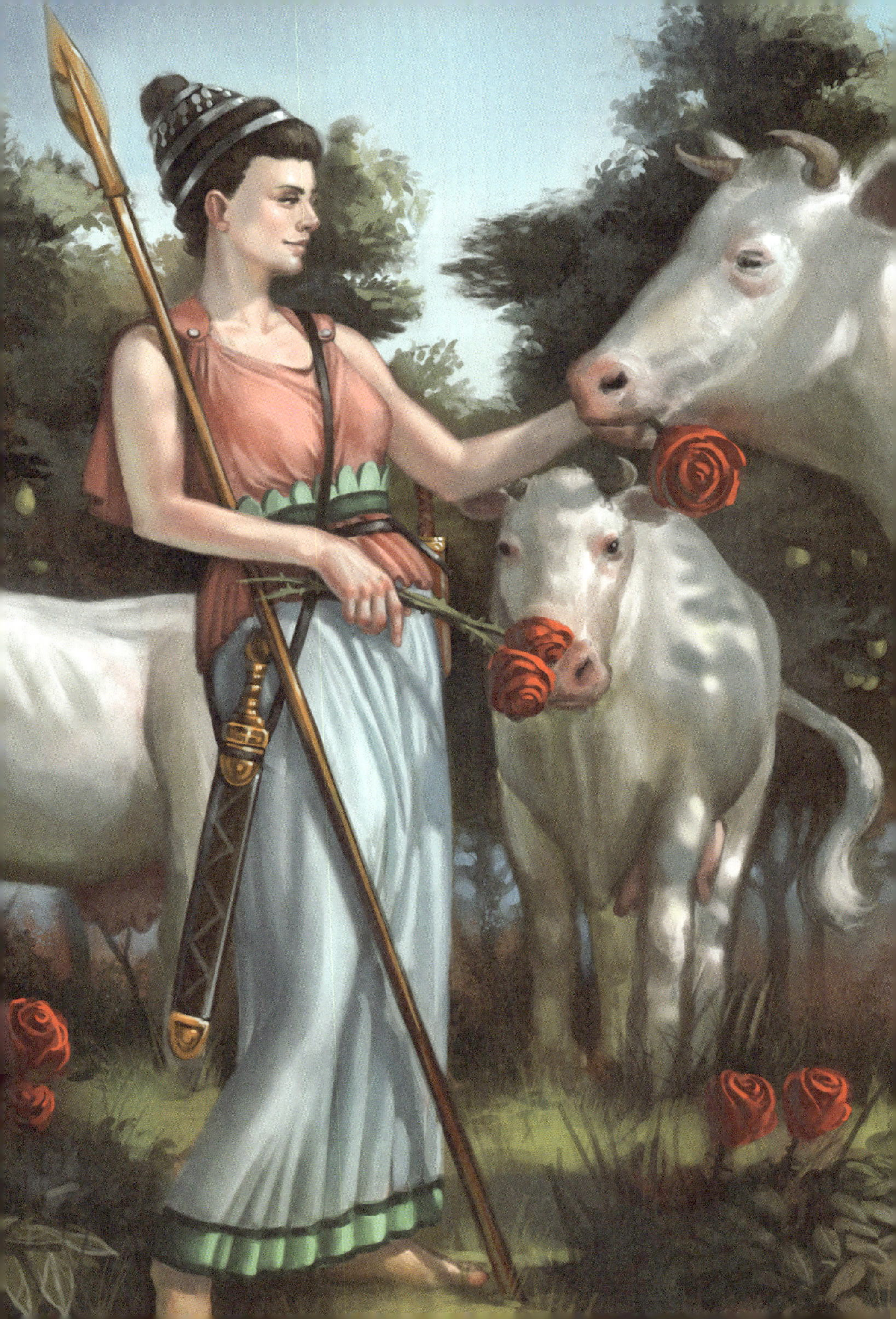

incandescence. Persons within the temple must make a saving throw each minute or lose 1 point of wisdom and be drawn towards the flame. A successful saving throw allows one to flee outside the temple, where lost wisdom is instantly restored. If such a person ever re-enters the temple, his wisdom reverts to its lower score. A man will throw himself into the column of fire, incinerating himself (or being swept into an alien celestial dimension, at the Referee's option), if his wisdom drops below 3.

1807 The Fire Wizard, a 5th-level magic-user (armor: none, hd 5, hp 10, move 120') dwells in a cave in which is a 30' diameter pool of lava. Not only is he unbothered by the oppressive heat, but he is healed 1 hp for each turn that he bathes in the lava. He can command the lava to splash any number of people within the cave, causing 8d6 points of damage (save for half) to each victim. The Fire Wizard can also cause a small fire to flame within his hands.

1808 A meticulously painted stone statue depicts a man with black hair and beard. He wears an archaic scholar's robe of deep purple. He holds a large bowl in his left hand and a vial in his right. Up to 100 coins may be placed in the large bowl. When this is done, the statue will pour a fizzing, white liquid from the vial upon the coins. Copper coins have an equal chance of turning to lead or to silver, silver coins to copper or to electrum, electrum coins to silver or to gold, gold coins to electrum or to platinum, and platinum coins turn to gold or double in number. The statue can transmute coins only once per week.

1809 A notorious gambler has drunkenly whispered to a few friends in this town (population 1,700) that he has struck it rich with the help of "a flinty old schoolmaster" somewhere to the north (cf. hex 1808).

Hex Descriptions

1810 On the ground lies a red-gold ring set with a large, smoldering purple gem. Both the metal of the ring and its stone are of unknown type. Smashing the gem will utterly banish from the earth the bipedal panda in hex 1812.

1811 A statue of a bearded, middle-aged man will truthfully answer one question per week. It will answer additional questions only if the questioner answers a riddle. A correct answer to the riddle will yield a correct answer from the statue, while an incorrect answer will yield an incorrect answer from the statue.

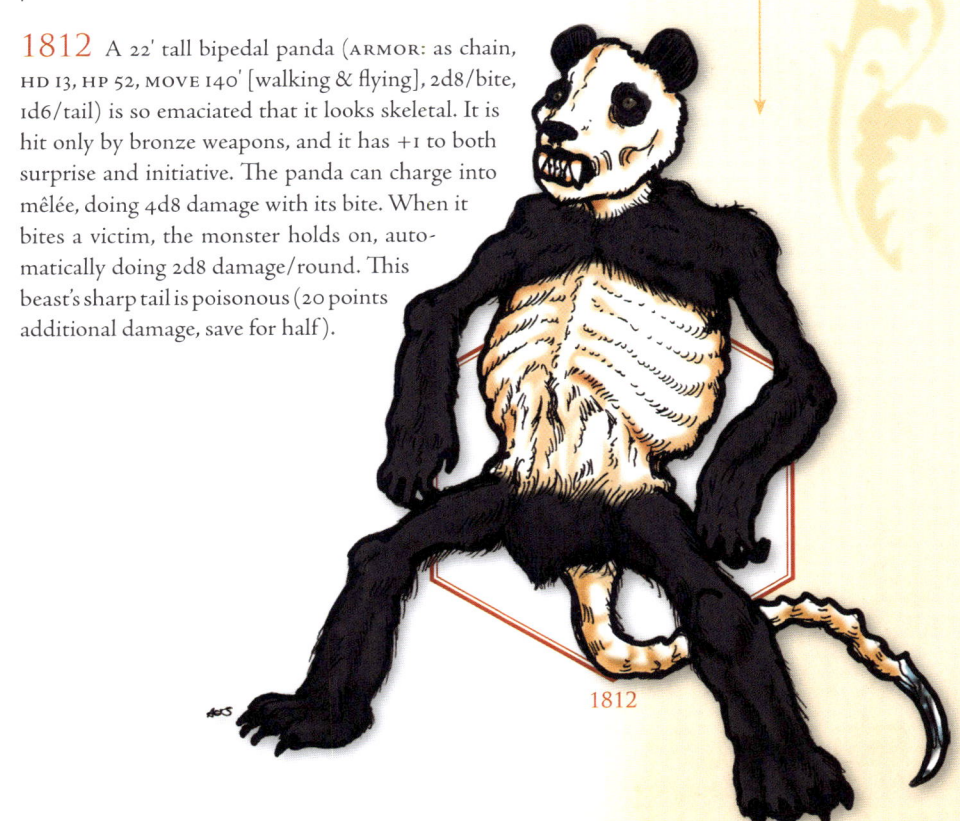

1812 A 22' tall bipedal panda (ARMOR: as chain, HD 13, HP 52, MOVE 140' [walking & flying], 2d8/bite, 1d6/tail) is so emaciated that it looks skeletal. It is hit only by bronze weapons, and it has +1 to both surprise and initiative. The panda can charge into mêlée, doing 4d8 damage with its bite. When it bites a victim, the monster holds on, automatically doing 2d8 damage/round. This beast's sharp tail is poisonous (20 points additional damage, save for half).

ISLE OF THE UNKNOWN

1813 A 6' tall wolf-man (ARMOR: none, HD 5, HP 24, MOVE 90', 1d10/bite) slithers upon the ground, moving itself with its arms. From its head grow deer antlers.

1814 Over the years, many handsome young men have returned to town (population 4,100) after an absence of weeks. Their jealous wives and lovers know only that it has to do with some hussy in the castle to the east (hex 1915).

1815 A 7' tall bipedal aardvark (ARMOR: as leather, HD 15, HP 68, MOVE 120', 1d8+1/tongue, 1d6 tail) can become a living shadow (surprise 5 in 6). While in this form it cannot attack. It regenerates 3 HP/round. The aardvark-man's fur changes like a chameleon (invisible when not moving). Its tongue also causes paralysis for 3d4 rounds (save avoids), while its tail is poisonous (20 points additional damage, save at +2 for half). This monster's gaze acts as a *Slow* spell, while instead of melee attacks it can fire either of the following rays from its eyes: fear (2d4 rounds) or stun (1d4+1 rounds).

1902 An 11' tall statue is made of glossy black stone. It holds a 10' long two-handed sword. If a chaotic character touches it, he will have +5 to hit and to damage in his next combat. Nothing happens if a neutral character touches the sword. If a lawful character touches it, the statue will attack (ARMOR: as plate + shield, HD 15, HP 68, MOVE 60', 8d8/sword).

1903 A giant boar (ARMOR: as leather + shield, HD 12, HP 51, MOVE 140', 1d10/tusks, 1d8/tail) is the size of a hippopotamus. Its body shimmers with kaleidoscopic colors. If the creature rolls a to hit score of 20 (or at least 4 more than needed to hit) for its tusk attack, the damage is 3d10.

1904 A round, 6" diameter, silvered mirror lies partially buried in the ground. When reflecting nature, the

HEX DESCRIPTIONS

1905

image in the mirror appears 12 hours different (i.e., 3 pm appears as 3 am, noon appears as midnight, etc.). This in no way allows one to peer into the past or into the future. The image is but a seeming.

1905 Orchids of myriad sorts grow from the rumps of the squirrels, chipmunks, mice, and rabbits that proliferate in these woods.

1813

85

ISLE OF THE UNKNOWN

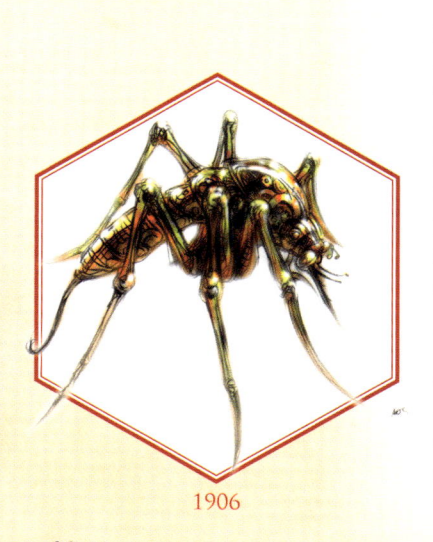

1906 A flightless, clockwork mosquito (ARMOR: as plate + shield, HD 11, HP 49, MOVE 55', 1d10/bite, 1d6 tail) has a thin, 30' long body. It can crawl upon walls or ceilings as easily as upon the ground. It is partially out-of-phase with the universe, and thus focusing upon it is difficult. This results in each foe's first attack against it automatically missing, and all further attacks are at −1, and all its saving throws are at +2. Only wooden weapons can hurt it, and it has only a 1 in 20 chance of being surprised. If the mosquito's roll to hit with its bite is a 20 (or at least 4 over what is needed to hit), then the bite does an additional 1d6 points of damage. Its tail also drains 1d6 points of wisdom (which return at the rate of 1 per hour). This mechanical monster can generate a 20' radius circle of fear (which makes those who fail their saving throw flee from the creature for 2d4 rounds), and the fear circle can be centered up to 80' away from the mosquito.

1907 A white marble statue of a 6' tall man holds a golden ram's fleece in his arms, and he has a spear strapped upon his back. Lawful and neutral humans who embrace the fleece will be healed of all ailments (all hit points restored, diseases cured, blind eyes opened, maimed limbs restored, etc.) other than age and death. Those who attempt to steal the fleece will take 2d12 points of damage upon touching it, and 2d12 points of damage each round that it is in their possession. Such miscreants can never thereafter benefit from the fleece's power. In addition, if a would-be thief does more than merely touch the fleece, the statue will attack (ARMOR: as plate + shield, HD 11, 50 HP, MOVE 40', 2d10/spear).

1908 Two identical marble statues of matrons stand 6' apart, holding 6' by 4' mirrors facing each other. Anyone who steps between the mirrors will become trapped in a mirror (save avoids), unable to escape, cast spells, or even speak. The reflection of such a victim will be seen peering out from the mirror. Death results

1906

HEX DESCRIPTIONS

if the mirror in which he is entrapped is destroyed. Destroying the opposite mirror accomplishes nothing. Only covering the opposite mirror with a blanket, cloak, etc. will free the prisoner. If the opposite mirror is destroyed, it must be replaced and then the new mirror covered in order to free anyone trapped.

1909 A gray stone statue is of an Amazon, clothed in a loincloth, holding a short bow, and girt with a quiver and a long sword scabbard. If any males come within short bow range, the statue will animate (ARMOR: as plate + shield, HD 14, HP 63, MOVE 120', 1d10/arrow, 2d10/sword) and attempt to slay them. When animated, the statue appears fully human, with coppery-red skin and black hair. She will not attack females unless attacked by them. Even then, the statue will concentrate on her female attackers only after all males in range are dead.

1910 A graceful aspen tree bends under the weight of a fallen ponderosa pine which lightning struck. If anyone comes within 12' of the aspen, it will entreat him in a whispery, feminine voice to move the fallen tree off of the aspen. The pine is small enough that a single man may accomplish the task. He who does so will have his charisma permanently raised by 1 point.

1911 A statue of rose-hued stone depicts a nude woman with long, black hair. Within 1 mile of the statue, Spring reigns eternal. No snows fall, and a gently warm, perfumed air wafts over the flowers filling the meadow. Hit points heal twice as fast in this area.

1912 In a clearing stands a 10' tall bronze statue of a muscular man clad in a loincloth. Waves of pain emanate from the statue. Anyone coming within 90' of the statue will feel pangs shoot through his body, causing 1 HP damage for each round spent within range. The statue is indestructible by means of normal weapons or standard spells. If anyone attempts to thus damage the statue, he must make a saving throw or suffer the damage intended for the statue.

1913 The sun never sets in a meadow of bright yellow flowers including sunflowers, marigolds, and celandine. Bay laurel, walnut, palm, and various types of citrus fruit trees dot the meadow. A dozen peaceful African lions with bright, almost metallic fur, roam freely. The master of this summerland is a 10th-level magic-user (ARMOR: as chain + shield, HD 9+1, HP 23, MOVE 120') who wears golden-yellow garments over a breastplate of gold. He also wears a golden ring set with a ruby. The lions (ARMOR: as 8, HD 5, HP 25, 20, 29, 22, 16, 21, 30, 17, 20, 29, 28, 31, MOVE 180', 1d12/bite, 1d6/two claws) will defend the magic-user, who can transform his head into that of a great, male lion (2d8/bite). In this shape he can shoot beams of intense sunlight from his eyes (range equal to that of a long bow) that cause 6d10 points of damage (save for half). Anyone reduced to 0 or fewer HP by the eyebeams will turn into a citrus fruit tree with particularly succulent fruits. The golden breastplate and ring will turn to lead if taken from the meadow, and the ruby into worthless glass.

1914 Within this thick forest, sounds as of children laughing and celebrating resound about 250' distant. The merriment ceases whenever a man approaches, only to resume a minute later 250' away. After the third interruption of the voices, they will fall silent for the next 24 hours.

1915 The slender turrets of a small white castle rise into the sky. This is the opulently-furnished residence of a seductive enchantress, a 4th-level magic-user (ARMOR: none, HD 4, HP 14, MOVE 120'). Her long raven hair alone clothes her. No man can possibly attack her, and a woman can do so only after making a saving throw at −3. She will direct her wiles upon any young

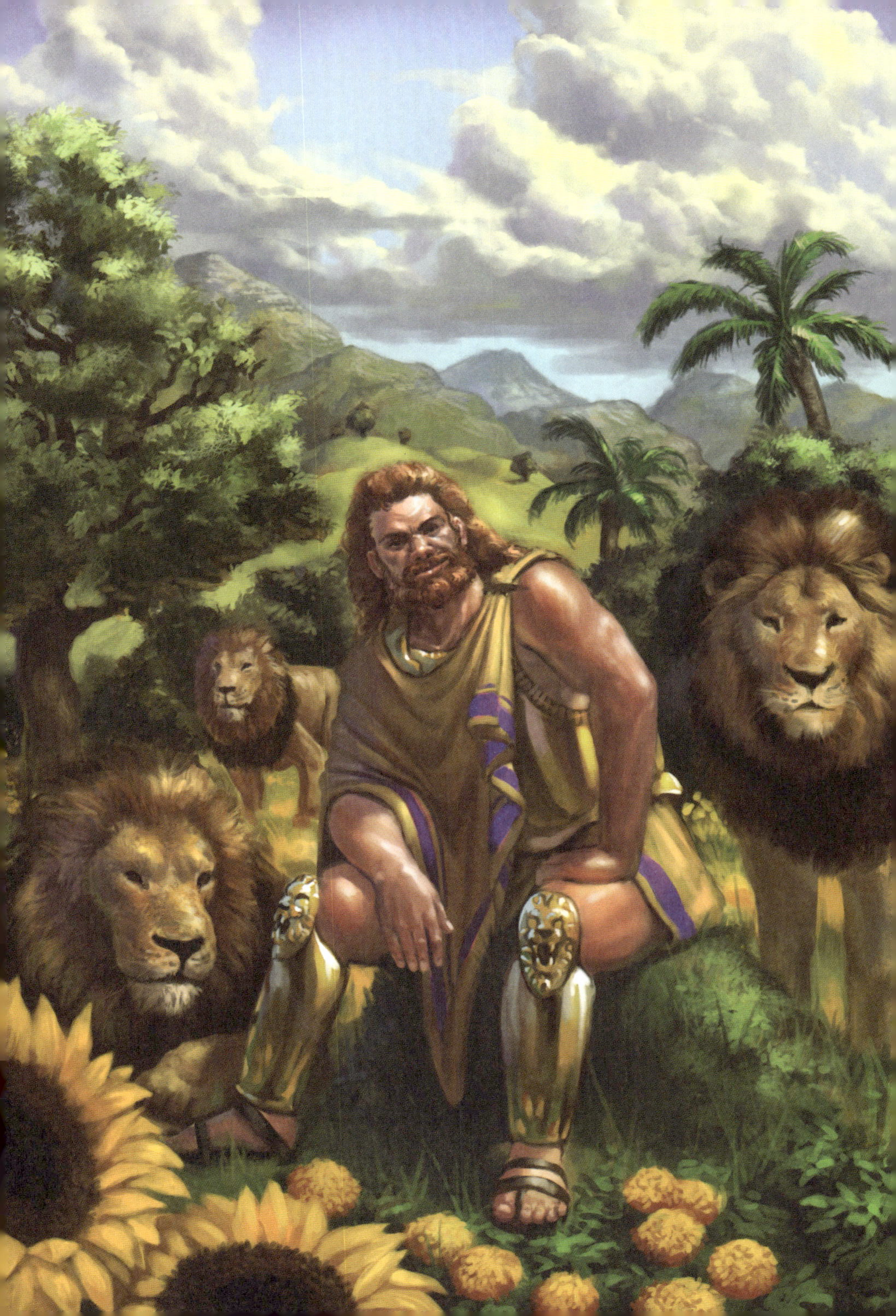

man with a charisma of 13 or higher. If such men fail a saving throw, they become her smitten slaves, receiving a new saving throw every week. Those enchanted by her will do anything unbloody for her, and will give their lives in her defense. The enchantress has two pet leopards (ARMOR: none, HD 4, HP 24, 12, MOVE 240', 1d8/bite, 1d4/two claws).

2001 A 5th-level cleric (ARMOR: plate + shield, HD 5, HP 20, MOVE 60') in a red surcoat bearing a white cross is the guardian of a saint's shrine. While armed with a broad sword and a war hammer, the cleric's primary weapons are the two gargoyles he has carved. Any attempted desecration of the shrine or an attack on the cleric or any pilgrim will cause the hideously-visaged statues (ARMOR: as plate + shield, HD 8, HP 34, 28, MOVE 180' [fly], 90' [walk], 3d6/two claws) to animate and attack.

2002 A noble huntsman in this town (population 2,200) busies himself with outfitting a party to hunt the giant rainbow boar seen in the forest (hex 1903). He especially covets its pelt.

2003 Four crystals (about 2' in diameter) of almost transparent smoky quartz tower 50' high. They always feel nearly as cold as ice. Their faded enchantment makes those who touch them wish to contemplate them unceasingly, though anyone can tear his attention away with no more harm than a feeling of regret.

2004 An invisible boulder sits in a depression in a clearing of the forest. Touching it will reveal it to be an irregularly shaped, roughly 10' diameter basalt boulder. Whenever human flesh ceases to touch the boulder, it turns invisible again.

2005 A 220 lb. crab (ARMOR: as plate + shield, HD 11, HP 62, MOVE 130' [walk & flight], 2d4/two claws)

HEX DESCRIPTIONS

has poisonous (12 points additional damage, save at +1 for half) bill-guisarmes in place of claws. It can also fire two bony projectiles (with the same range as a short bow) that cause 1d6 damage each. The crab can change its color to match its surroundings, which makes if effectively invisible when over 50' away, and gives it a +2 in 6 chance to surprise (while it is surprised only 1 in 12). It reflects 1st-level offensive spells back at the caster. Further, only five spells can affect it: *Chaos*, *Light*, *Power Word Stun*, *Prismatic Wall*, and *Telekinesis*. It can at will change into a liquid, and in this state it can neither attack nor be attacked by physical weapons. Lastly, when in total darkness (in which the creature can see perfectly), the crab's bill-guisarmes do 3d6 damage when its attack roll is a natural 20 (or at least 4 over the score needed).

2006 A forest of hazel and walnut trees enjoys year-round warmth. Yellow blossoms (azaleas, lilies-of-the-valley, myrtle, etc.) fill the air with a pleasant lemon scent. Small yellow songbirds, butterflies, and chattering monkeys play amongst the trees. Two twins of youthful mien live in this paradise. Each is an 11th-level magic-user (ARMOR: none, HD 9+2, HP 35, MOVE 120') with identical abilities. If attacked, weapons and armor of living mercury will flow from their bodies, giving them an armor class equivalent to plate + shield. Each can strike twice per round with his weapons (of whatever sort desired), and the weapons will do thrice the damage of a normal weapon. Once per day, each brother can create an identical image of a person and make it attack the original person. The image will have identical abilities and equipment to the original.

2007 A 2' high crack in the side of the mountain leads 40' to a cave system of Lechuguilla-like loveliness. In the first chamber stands a statue of a bearded man hewn of gray stone, holding a small hammer. Anyone touching this statue will be overwhelmed with a desire to never leave the enchanting caverns (save applies). Humans of 1st level or higher can try another saving throw every week, though at −1 the first week, at −2 the second week, etc. Humans of 0-level are allowed only a single saving throw. Deeper in the caverns are twenty-two 0-level humans who live within, chipping the rock only to open up entrances to further chambers. Their crystalline lamps make the underground paradise glitter with untold beauties.

2008 A graybeard lives alone in the forest in a wooden house. Above his fireplace hangs a mechanical clock with 15 numbers on its face and three hands: an hour hand, a minute hand, and an inscrutable hand which sometimes stops or even goes backwards. Though the old man effortlessly understands the clock, others can

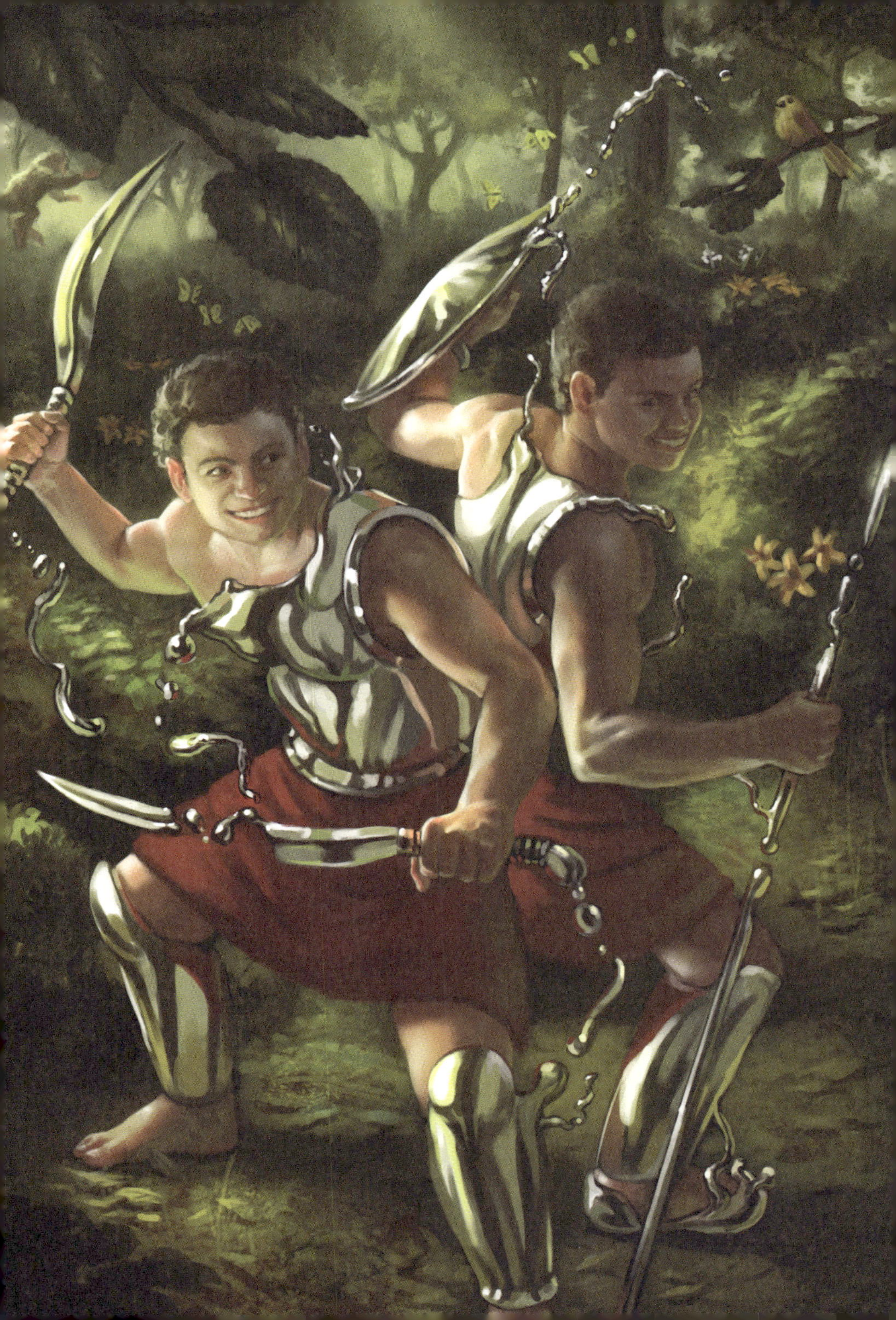

make no sense of his explanations involving sideways time, multi-dimensional time, inside-out time, etc.

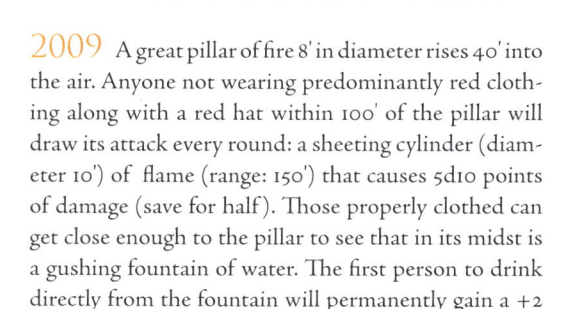

2009 A great pillar of fire 8' in diameter rises 40' into the air. Anyone not wearing predominantly red clothing along with a red hat within 100' of the pillar will draw its attack every round: a sheeting cylinder (diameter 10') of flame (range: 150') that causes 5d10 points of damage (save for half). Those properly clothed can get close enough to the pillar to see that in its midst is a gushing fountain of water. The first person to drink directly from the fountain will permanently gain a +2 bonus to all saving throws against fire and heat. To do this requires the armor found in hex 0816.

2010 This gray stone statue depicts an old, bearded man in a voluminous robe. Any magic-user who touches it will seemingly experience nothing. In the next combat in which he attempts to cast a spell, however, he will discover that his spell repertoire is either 3 levels higher or 3 levels lower (50% chance of either) for that combat only.

2011 A 30' long serpentine plant-stalk (ARMOR: none, HD 3, HP 19, MOVE 90', 1d10/thorns) is covered with thorns that appear to have blood dripping from them, but this blood is illusory. This monster is immune to lightning.

2012 Several people in town (population 1,600) have visited the outskirts of a meadow to the southwest in which African lions roam and the sun never sets (hex 1913).

2013 In this pleasant meadow, an innumerable amount of weapons (swords, bows, arrows, spears, morning stars, etc.) covers the ground in a 40' diameter circle. In the midst of this circle is a statue, realistically hued, of two nude women (one blonde and the

Hex Descriptions

other raven-haired) from the Isle of Lesbos. If anyone touches any of the weapons, or if he enters the 40' diameter circle, he will discard all his weapons (no saving throw). He is then free to touch the statue, which will send torrents of ecstasy through him. This boon can be gained by any given person but once each year.

2014 Large and delicious white mushrooms speckle the forest floor. Anyone eating a mushroom will physically age 10 years (save avoids). The additional years will fall away at the rate of 1 year for every week that passes.

2015 When a man sees a bare, rocky hillock, out of nothingness an aspen with yellow-gold fall foliage will appear upon the top of the hillock. Leaves from the tree float gently to the ground. When viewers move at least 100' away from the hillock and turn away, the aspen will vanish. The tree can appear no more than thrice in a day.

2103 In the taverns of this town (population 1,800) one can hear of the towering, ice-cold crystals to the west (hex 2003).

2104 A man-sized quadrupedal leek plant (ARMOR: none, HD 15, HP 71, MOVE none, 2d10/envelop) is always in gaseous form. It is thus immune to weapons, but spells affect it. If anyone approaches within 110', it fires a 45° cone of deafness (lasts 2d4 turns). Those approaching within 80' lose 1 point of strength every 3 rounds (1 point returns per hour). It is poisonous to the touch (20 points of damage, save at +2 for half). Anyone daring to come within a yard of this abomination will be enveloped, which also causes total memory loss (including spells). Memory can be returned only by dispel magic or remove curse.

2104

ISLE OF THE UNKNOWN

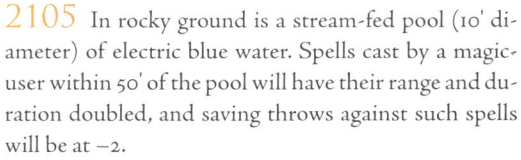

2105 In rocky ground is a stream-fed pool (10' diameter) of electric blue water. Spells cast by a magic-user within 50' of the pool will have their range and duration doubled, and saving throws against such spells will be at −2.

2106 This monster looks like a 280 lb. American Burmese domestic cat (ARMOR: as plate + shield, HD 13, HP 65, MOVE 160', 1d10/bite) with metallic fur. The feline is immune to all mental attacks and to all mundane weapons. Its cat-eyes allow it to see anything invisible. Poison (20 points additional damage, save at −1 for half damage) drips from its fangs. The cat can make 2d6 foes glow at a time, which gives them a −2 penalty to armor class.

2107 A 6th-level cleric (ARMOR: plate + shield, HD 6, HP 36, MOVE 60'), garbed in a red surcoat with a white cross, rides northeast upon his horse. He is armed with a broad sword, mace, dagger, and a long bow (with 24 arrows). He has the divine gift of doing maximum damage with each of his successful attacks. The cleric is on a quest to destroy the monster in hex 2303.

2108 A four-legged kangaroo (ARMOR: as chain, HD 5, HP 13, MOVE 130' [fly], 1d8/kick, 1d6/stinger) is the size of a cow and can move only by flying, in spite of its lack of wings. Shark-like fins grow from its body. The barbed stinger that grows from the tip of its tail snags in its victim, automatically doing damage each round thereafter. At the beginning of each round, the monster regains 2 HP, even if brought below 0 HP. Only damage from spells does not regenerate.

2109 A man-sized flea (ARMOR: as chain + shield, HD 1, HP 5, MOVE 140' [swim only], 2d8/bite) sports deer-like antlers on its head. The insect never leaves the water.

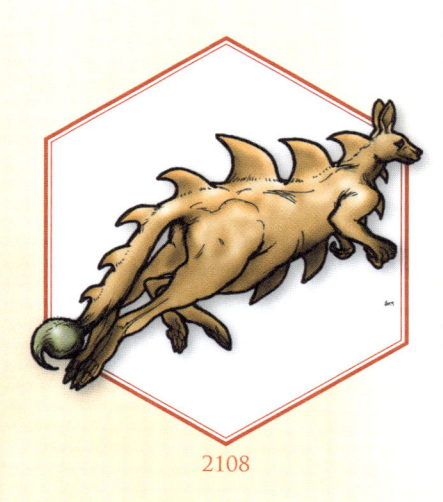

HEX DESCRIPTIONS

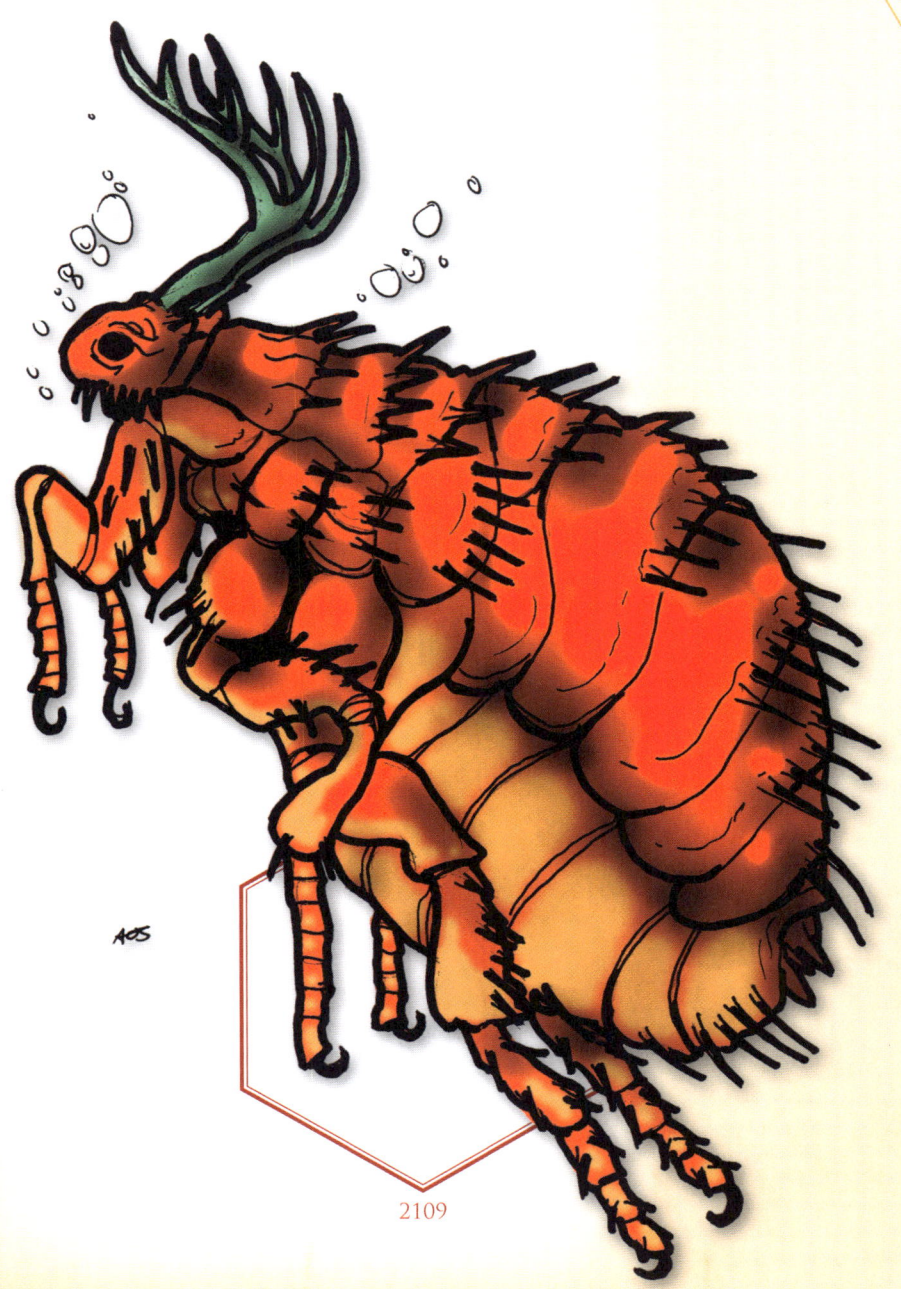

2109

2109

97

ISLE OF THE UNKNOWN

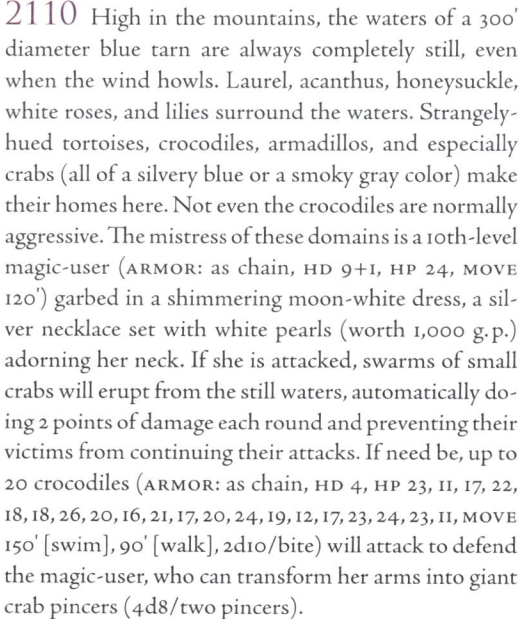

2110 High in the mountains, the waters of a 300' diameter blue tarn are always completely still, even when the wind howls. Laurel, acanthus, honeysuckle, white roses, and lilies surround the waters. Strangely-hued tortoises, crocodiles, armadillos, and especially crabs (all of a silvery blue or a smoky gray color) make their homes here. Not even the crocodiles are normally aggressive. The mistress of these domains is a 10th-level magic-user (ARMOR: as chain, HD 9+1, HP 24, MOVE 120') garbed in a shimmering moon-white dress, a silver necklace set with white pearls (worth 1,000 g.p.) adorning her neck. If she is attacked, swarms of small crabs will erupt from the still waters, automatically doing 2 points of damage each round and preventing their victims from continuing their attacks. If need be, up to 20 crocodiles (ARMOR: as chain, HD 4, HP 23, 11, 17, 22, 18, 18, 26, 20, 16, 21, 17, 20, 24, 19, 12, 17, 23, 24, 23, 11, MOVE 150' [swim], 90' [walk], 2d10/bite) will attack to defend the magic-user, who can transform her arms into giant crab pincers (4d8/two pincers).

2111 An 8' long monster (ARMOR: as leather, HD 3, HP 11, MOVE 240' [fly], 90' [slither], 1d6/beak) has no legs, a serpentine body covered with orange and yellow feathers, and the head of a hawk.

2112 A man-sized monster (ARMOR: as plate, HD 5, HP 29, MOVE 130', 1d8/bite, 1d6/tail) looks like a slightly elongated raspberry with vaguely lizard-like head, tail, and four legs, all raspberry-like in color and texture.

2113 A 30' high waterfall, bounding down stepped rock, will magically deafen for 1 day anyone who comes within 40' and hears it (unless a saving throw is made). Deafened spell-casters have a 90% chance of spell failure because of the difficulty of properly pronouncing their words.

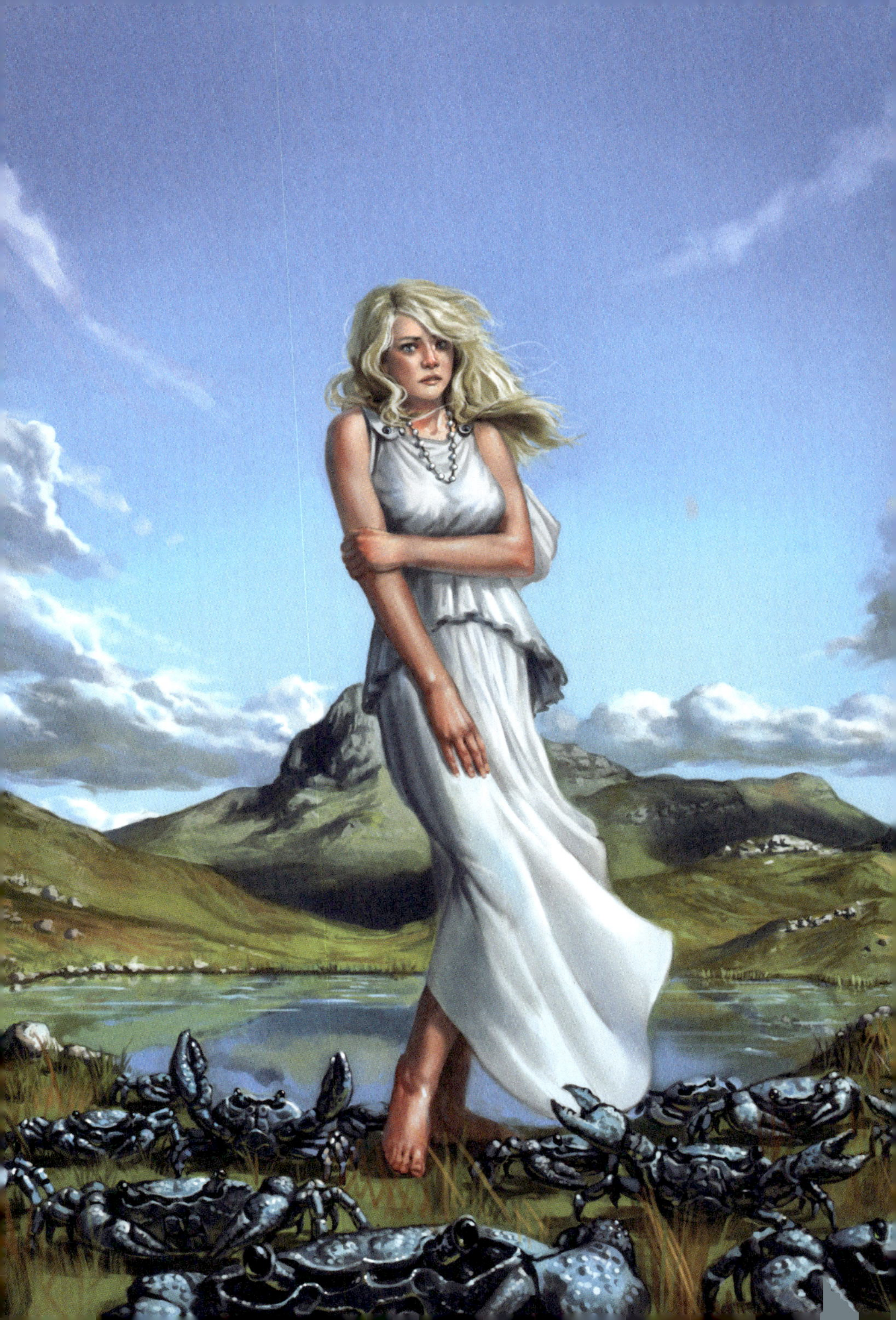

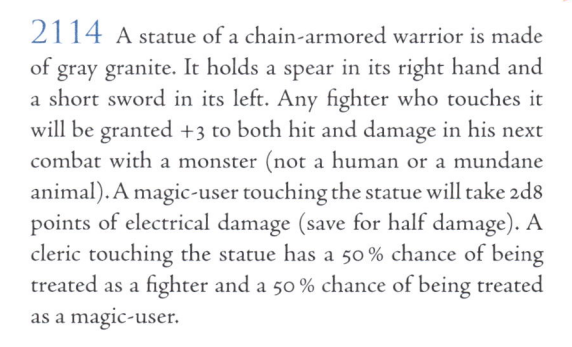

2114 A statue of a chain-armored warrior is made of gray granite. It holds a spear in its right hand and a short sword in its left. Any fighter who touches it will be granted +3 to both hit and damage in his next combat with a monster (not a human or a mundane animal). A magic-user touching the statue will take 2d8 points of electrical damage (save for half damage). A cleric touching the statue has a 50% chance of being treated as a fighter and a 50% chance of being treated as a magic-user.

2115 A 6' tall bipedal monster (ARMOR: as plate + shield, HD 6, HP 32, MOVE 360' [fly], 120' [walk], 1d6/bite, 1d6/projectiles) has a toothed maw, its body is entirely covered with iridescent feathers and scales, and it possesses hummingbird wings. Its body is perpetually soaked so as to drip water and leaves a wet trail wherever it goes. It thus takes only half damage from fire or heat (magical or otherwise). It can shoot sharp scales from its body with the range of a short bow. Short vines grow from its body, and orange berries grow from the vines. Anyone who eats these berries will become confused and do one of the following for 2d8 rounds: 1) attack nearest creature, 2) stand perfectly still, 3) run in a random direction, or 4) attack his friends.

2202 A statue of brown-green stone depicts a hunter armed with a bow, an arrow held in the string. Touching the arrowhead will either transform the person into a brown bearmelee or into a mink (50% chance of either) for 24 hours. The polymorphed person retains his intellect, but will not be able to speak.

2203 A 210 lb. frog (ARMOR: as shield, HD 1, HP 5, MOVE 140', 1d10/bite, 1d4/two claws) is equally adept at moving on either four legs or on two. While unintelligent, it can imitate human speech in a manner similar to parrots. When encountered, it will repeat in a sobbing voice, "No! No! Somebody help me! No!"

HEX DESCRIPTIONS 2203

ISLE OF THE UNKNOWN

2204 A grotesquery (ARMOR: as plate, HD 7, HP 25, MOVE 140' [jumping], 1d8/bite, 1d4/tail, 1d6/projectile leaf) when still looks like a misshapen, leafy elm log. When the horrid thing moves, its lizard-like body, beaver-tail, and distorted head (with features of both lizard and beaver) become apparent. Worst of all, in combat it sweats large amounts of blood. The monster can shoot its razor-sharp leaves with the same range as a short bow.

2205 An alabaster statue of an armored warrior woman holds a spear in her right hand, and an ivory owl (worth 100 g.p.) perches upon her left. The owl can easily be removed from the statue. A person will gain 1 point of wisdom if he does no more than gently touch the owl. This gift can be gained only once by any given person, and it will be granted no more than once every three months. If the owl is taken, three hours later the thief will lose both 1 point of wisdom and the owl, which magically reappears on the statue's hand.

2206 A complete cycle of the four seasons occurs every day in a small woodland of aspen and oak. In a matter of hours, a person can witness the trees bud with leaves, which grow large and green, then turn red and gold and fall to the ground, etc. Spring arrives at 3 a.m., summer at 9 a.m., fall at 3 p.m., and winter at 9 p.m.

2207 On the mountaintop dwells a solitary 5th-level cleric (ARMOR: plate + shield, HD 5, HP 36, MOVE 120') who has been granted the gifts of skin as hard as steel and imperviousness to the elements. He needs not food, drink, nor sleep, and he devotes his hours to celestial contemplation. In combat he wields a two-handed sword that miraculously appears in his hands. Any time the dice indicate that the cleric will take damage, he gets to roll a saving throw to avoid it altogether.

HEX DESCRIPTIONS

2208 A weathered white statue of a warrior in a loincloth holding a short sword stands alone in a clearing. If a character steps on the statue's shadow (20% chance per character coming within 6' of the statue), the shadow attacks (MOVE 120', 3d4/sword). The shadow cannot be directly harmed. Destroying the statue (100 hit points) will dissipate the shadow.

2209 High above tree line in a flowery meadow stands a hydrangea that grows hundreds of literal snowballs instead of blossoms. They are unusually refreshing if eaten, and each one will heal 1d8+1 points of fire or heat damage.

2210 In the midst of a deep forest stands a jade statue of a curly-haired bearded man clothed only with a rude animal skin and a wreath of leaves upon his head. If anyone attempts to molest the statue, the trees of the surrounding forest will sluggishly animate and attack, automatically causing 1d6 points of damage per round to everyone within 100' of the statue. The trees will allow victims to flee, but they are so numerous and mighty that they cannot possibly be defeated in mêlée. The statue has a 30% chance of being destroyed if anyone decides to clear the forest with a fireball.

2211 An 8' tall statue of a muscular and bearded man wearing only a lion pelt is hewn from white marble. If a man touches the lion pelt, it will (50% chance) turn into a *Smilodon* (ARMOR: as leather, HD 8, HP 55, MOVE 180', 3d6/bite, 2d4/two claws) and attack or (50% chance) bestow upon the man the ability to turn himself into a Smilodon one combat per day for 3d10 days. Only one person can possess this ability at one time.

2212 A 180 lb. creature (ARMOR: as shield, HD 11, HP 48, MOVE 120' [walk and swim], 1d6+1/claw, 1d6/tail) is a deer with a fur-covered serpentine body with four tiny legs. Only silver weapons can hurt it. Each success-

2212

103

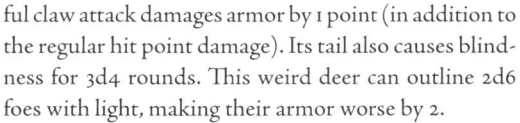

ful claw attack damages armor by 1 point (in addition to the regular hit point damage). Its tail also causes blindness for 3d4 rounds. This weird deer can outline 2d6 foes with light, making their armor worse by 2.

2213 A 16' tall humanoid oriole (ARMOR: as leather + shield, HD 8, HP 39, MOVE 240' [fly], 140' [walk], 1d10/two spear-hands) has two arms that end in spears. It can be hit only by bronze weapons and is immune to cutting attacks. The monster regenerates 1 HP/round. All invisible creatures or objects can be seen by the bird-man. Also, it can turn itself into a liquid, in which state it can neither attack nor be attacked by physical means.

2214 A statue is hewn of a rich, creamy-gold stone. It is of a nude woman holding a small jar tipped towards the earth. Out of the jar pours real honey, which vanishes an inch above the ground. If eaten, the honey will heal 1d8 points of damage. Any given person can be healed only once per day.

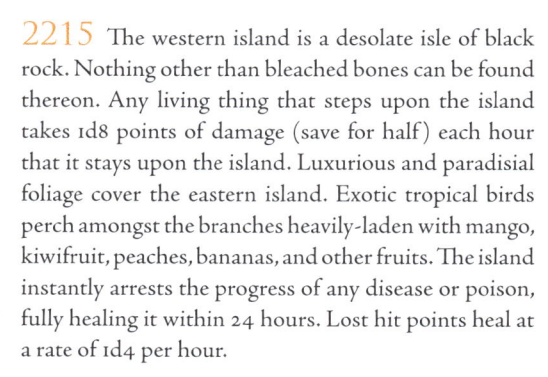

2215 The western island is a desolate isle of black rock. Nothing other than bleached bones can be found thereon. Any living thing that steps upon the island takes 1d8 points of damage (save for half) each hour that it stays upon the island. Luxurious and paradisial foliage cover the eastern island. Exotic tropical birds perch amongst the branches heavily-laden with mango, kiwifruit, peaches, bananas, and other fruits. The island instantly arrests the progress of any disease or poison, fully healing it within 24 hours. Lost hit points heal at a rate of 1d4 per hour.

2303 An 18' tall albino frog-man (ARMOR: as leather, HD 10, HP 42, MOVE 140' [hopping and levitating], 2d6+2/bite, 2d4/tail) is immune to fire and can levitate as long as it is within 10' of a solid surface. If it rolls a 20 (or 4 more than needed to hit) with a bite attack, its

HEX DESCRIPTIONS

bite does an additional 1d8 points of damage. It can fire from its pink eyes a 140′ long cone with a 45° arc that drains 1 point of constitution. Lost points return at a rate of 1 per hour.

2304 Thick growths of dying, rotten cactus choke the black soil, from which grow white lichen and rust-colored grasses. An odor of decay fills the air. The cacti themselves have swollen into abominable shapes unlike any mundane cacti. Pale green vipers with bright ochre eyes live in holes in some of the cactus. Those foolish enough to disturb the vipers risk venomous bites (6 points of damage, save avoids). Long-legged insects the size of tarantulas and the color of decaying corpses infest the cactus forest. Though harmless, they emit a malodorous stench when crushed. They will follow for 1–3 miles those who leave the cactus forest.

2305 In a 100′ diameter grove of Aleppo pine stand nine stone statues of travelers. Anyone reaching the center of the grove will begin to take 1d8 points of damage (save for half) each round. Anyone reaching 0 or fewer HP will turn to stone.

2306 A 20′ tall monster (ARMOR: as chain, HD 5, HP 31, MOVE 140′ [walk and fly], 2d6/bite, 2d4/tail) has the body and tail of a salamander, with the legs and head of a fly. It is predominantly white, with bright orange mottles. Though it has six legs, it walks upon only two of them, except when it crawls upon walls or ceilings.

2307 A 7′ long bipedal bass (ARMOR: as shield, HD 9, HP 35, MOVE 90′, 1d8+1/claw, 1d6/tail) is essentially a fish-man with atrophied legs that slithers and pulls itself along the ground with its arms. It has a +2 initiative bonus, and it is immune to mind-affecting magic. The stinger in its tail is poisonous (18 points damage, save at +1 to avoid). This piscean horror can project a 90′ cone with a 45° arc. Those within the cone suffer −2

ISLE OF THE UNKNOWN

to saves, attack rolls, and armor for 1d4 turns, and their food and drink spoils.

2308 If anyone comes closer than 20' to a silver-plated statue of a nude woman, she will begin to sing an enchanting and ethereal air which will lull to sleep for 2d4 hours all who hear it (save avoids). Sleepers cannot be awakened.

2309 A 5' tall statue is of a merry young man playing a flute. His clothes are painted in a checkered pattern of

HEX DESCRIPTIONS

purple and yellow. If the statue is touched, or if a person stays more than 5 minutes within 10' of it, its flute emits an odd and humorous tune. Listeners failing a saving throw will caper and prance for 10 minutes, at the end of which both their intelligence and wisdom drop to 3. Lost points return at the rate of 1 per hour. Spell-use will be impossible until intelligence (for magic-users) or wisdom (for clerics) returns to normal.

2310 A hippopotamus-sized ladybug (ARMOR: as chain + shield, HD 3, HP 17, MOVE 140' [walk and swim], 1d12/bite) has transparent outer features, revealing its innards. All six of its legs end in suction cups, which the insect uses to walk along walls and ceilings.

2311 A statue of Medusa carved from black-green stone radiates a profound feeling of unease. To approach within 40' of it, one must make a saving throw or flee in fear for 5 minutes. With each additional 10' closer one wishes to go, he must make another saving throw or flee in fear. Thus, to actually touch the statue one must make 5 saving throws. If anyone fails a saving throw, he is unable to ever again come closer than 40' to the statue. If a person touches the statue, at any one time of his choice during the next year, his gaze will petrify (save allowed).

2312 Blue, green, and aqua bubbles (1' in diameter) float from the O-shaped mouth of a bas-relief of the Green Man carved upon an ancient, ruined wall. When any man approaches within 18', a deep and hollow voice booms from the face: "If you pop the bubbles, you'll be sorry!" The merest touch pops a bubble, thereby shrinking the person to 6" and transporting him inside a bubble (save avoids), which will pop 1d20+10 seconds later. When a 6" tall man falls to the ground, he will take damage as though he fell 40'. He then returns to normal size.

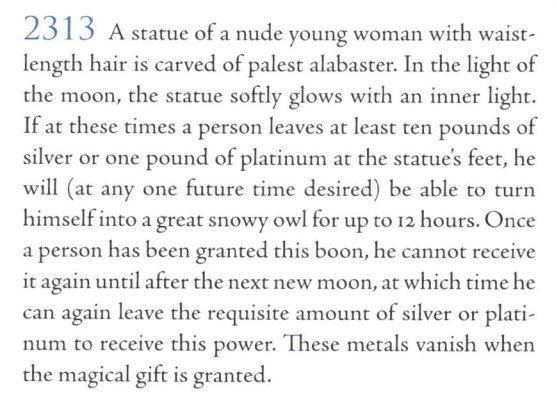

2313 A statue of a nude young woman with waist-length hair is carved of palest alabaster. In the light of the moon, the statue softly glows with an inner light. If at these times a person leaves at least ten pounds of silver or one pound of platinum at the statue's feet, he will (at any one future time desired) be able to turn himself into a great snowy owl for up to 12 hours. Once a person has been granted this boon, he cannot receive it again until after the next new moon, at which time he can again leave the requisite amount of silver or platinum to receive this power. These metals vanish when the magical gift is granted.

2314 Some years ago a wizard with a sardonic sense of humor transformed a young 2nd-level lawful cleric into a 14' tall bipedal gold pearlscale angelfish (ARMOR: as leather + shield, HD 5, HP 28, MOVE 140' [walk and fly], 1d12/bite). The transformed cleric uncontrollably acts as an aggressive monster. If returned to his rightful form, he will also regain his mental faculties. His divine gift as a cleric is as follows: Three times per day, with a 40% chance of success, he can pray for the manifestation of the intolerable geometric glory of a beneficent daimon. Any monster or diabolist will flee in terror for 3 turns (no saving throw) at the sight. Any other opponent will be unable to attack the cleric for the duration of the vision (7 minutes).

2315 Upon this garden-like island live two dozen castaways, the survivors of a merchant vessel and of a pirate ship. All are clad in tattered garments. Any human who stays upon the isle for more than a fortnight will have his lifespan increased to 1,000 years. (In fact, none of the inhabitants is under 300 years old.) Those who stay for longer than a fortnight will instinctively know that immediate death awaits if they go more than 300' from the shores. Any attempt at violence against a human on the island will cause the attacker to fall unconscious for 1 hour, thus making it impossible to

HEX DESCRIPTIONS

attack others. The inhabitants are carefree, welcoming, and open about the nature of the island.

2316 A mighty statue (25' tall) of jade-green stone depicts a crowned sea king. It stands on a 20' diameter rock 1 mile north of the shore of the small island. If a ship comes closer than 1 mile to the island, the sea will churn with a fierce wind, which has an 80% chance of sinking the ship. The sandy island has plenty of fruit, fish, fowl, and fresh water. Wrecked ships and human skeletons litter the shores. Any attempt to leave the island by boat or ship will cause the same fierce winds.

2402 Three beasts (ARMOR: as leather, HD 4, HP 18, 19, 17, MOVE 40', 1d6/bite) are basically 4' long alligators with suction cups on their legs and 4" long maxillary canines. They can move along walls and ceilings as easily and swiftly as they can move on the ground. These monsters cannot abide humans. In combat they will first attack those wearing the least armor, and then those with the fewest remaining hit points.

2403 Within the white walls of the joyous castle of the Harvest Knight, 6d12 persons daily feast and make glad. The Harvest Knight, an 8th-level fighter (ARMOR: plate + shield, HD 8, HP 54, MOVE 60'), is the very soul of robust joviality. He wears rich robes of autumnal red, brown, and orange. His jewelry and that of his wife are resplendent with topaz, amber, and yellow-brown cairngorm. His horn, hight the Cornucopia, provides endless viands and choice red wine.

2404 A graceful white statue of a woman wearing a long, sleeveless gown has outstretched swan wings. Any lawful character who caresses the wings will be granted the ability to fly (240' speed) for one hour. This gift of flight can be used any time within the next month.

2405 An opulently furnished mansion overlooking the sea is the erstwhile home of a powerful enchanter. Therein stand the immobilized bodies of fifty young woman of surpassing grace and loveliness, their youth unnaturally made perpetual by the magical arts of their captor.

2406 Fourteen lizards (ARMOR: as leather, HD 7, HP 32, 30, 30, 28, 33, 31, 37, 28, 36, 33, 34, 26, 33, 34, MOVE 40', 1d4/bite, 1d6/sting) are between 2' and 3' in length. Their tails are tipped with stingers. These monsters attack each round with a bite and tail stinger. They prefer to attack spellcasters (magic-users before clerics). Otherwise they will attack whoever is closest. The creatures procreate by laying eggs inside dead humans, and they will therefore attack all humans they see. In addition to the normal damage, those struck by one of these monsters' tails will lose one point of wisdom (no saving throw). The lost point returns after 1 hour.

2407 A statue, carved of a fiery orange stone, depicts a youth. Its left arm has been broken off and is missing. If anyone touches the statue, he will take 2d6

HEX DESCRIPTIONS

points of heat damage (save for half). If this occurs, the statue will apologize and explain that he is unable to speak until someone touches him. The statue will ask for his arm to be returned to him, which is possessed by a collector of antiquities in the city in hex 2409. If the arm is returned, the statue will reveal the location in hex 1401 of an ancient cup of harlequin opal (worth 5,000 g.p.).

2408 A 7th-level cleric (ARMOR: plate +shield, HD 7, HP 35, MOVE 60') in a red surcoat with a white cross is mounting his horse. The charred bodies of 6 men lie upon the burned grass. In addition to arms of short sword, war hammer, and dagger, the cleric has the miraculous gift of calling down torrents of fire upon his foes (8d6 damage, save for half). He can also call upon a 30' high, 6' diameter pillar of fire that darts between the cleric and his foes. Anyone charging through it will take 12d6 damage (no save).

2409 The King of the Island rules from this city (population 19,100), which also serves as the episcopal see. Most clerics on the island are members of the order (signified by a red surcoat emblazoned with a white cross) attached to the city's hospital. Men of all types inhabit the city, and nearly any sort of good or service can be purchased here.

2410 A 15' tall woodpecker (ARMOR: as leather, HD 5, HP 22, MOVE 210' [fly], 130' [walk], 1d12/beak) is covered with open sores that ooze a clear slime. Anyone coming in contact with the slime will lose 1 point of strength. Lost strength pointsreturn at the rate of 1/hour. This monster gets a +1 bonus to its initiative rolls, and it takes only half damage from physical (non-magical) attacks. It can change itself into any inanimate object of its general size.

ISLE OF THE UNKNOWN

2411 A mounted 6th-level cleric (ARMOR: plate + shield, HD 6, HP 22+66, MOVE 60') serves devils. Armed with war hammer and battle axe, he wears the red surcoat with white cross of the holy order that he has infiltrated. The cleric gains 1 HP for every HD of human being that he corrupts to the black pleasures of diabolism. He has 66 HP in addition to his normal HP. These additional HP are not regained when lost.

2412 A 6' tall duck-man (ARMOR: as leather + shield, HD 7, HP 41, MOVE 150' [walk and fly], 1d8/beak) is immune to lightning. Once per combat it can generate 1d4+1 mirror images of itself. Once per turn it can generate a wall of fire up to 20' away in any configuration that is no more than 35 square feet. Anything coming into contact with the fire will take 7d4 points of damage (save for half). Strangest of all, this duck-man is actually a gate to the Demiplane of Ducks. Killing the being will open the gate.

2413 Verdigris coats a copper statue of an impish man sticking out his tongue. Anyone coming within 12' of the front of the statue will be sprayed by poison that causes 1d10 points of damage each round until a saving throw is made.

2414 A narrow cave mouth will barely allow a man to squeeze through. The cave itself forms a rough corridor 5' in diameter that dead-ends after 40'. Those leaving the cave will find themselves in an identical cave in hex 0411. A given person can teleport between the caves only once in his life.

2415 This rocky island with stands of pine trees is unremarkable, save for the fact that every 24 hours at the stroke of midnight, the island has a 25% chance of vanishing. Thus, every day the island has a 75% chance of existing, and a 25% chance of not existing. If a living creature is on the island when it vanishes, he will

HEX DESCRIPTIONS

subjectively experience nothing. When the island reappears, the creature will also reappear with no awareness that time has passed.

2505 This monster (ARMOR: as leather + shield, HD 8, HP 35, MOVE 210' [fly], 150' [walk], 1d10/beak, 1d8/tail) is invisible, even when attacking. If it is slain, its form will become visible: a hippopotamus-sized crane with a light covering of violet hair over its white plumage.

2507 In an ancient ruin the mosaic floor depicting a scholar or a wizard is still intact. This is actually the Tessellated Mage, a 6th-level magic-user (HP 17) who escaped death by melding himself into the mosaic. If anyone steps upon the mosaic, the tesserae will burst from the floor and swirl around and strike all those within the ruin for 6d6 points of damage per round (save for half). Every lost hit point will be absorbed by the Tessellated Mage, who requires human blood to continue his millennial existence. One absorbed hit point will vanish with the passing of each month, and he will die when his last hit point fades. The only way to directly destroy the mage is to pour acid upon the figure in the mosaic.

2512 A 14' tall amphibious carp-man (ARMOR: as leather, HD 14, HP 73, MOVE 130', 1d12+4/bite, 1d6/tail) is immune to lightning and to most weapons, though piercing attacks will cause half damage. No mundane animal can come within 10' of it, and it can glow at will with the radiance of a light spell. The carp-man's gaze drains 1d6 points of wisdom (which return 1 point/hour), and it can shoot dorsal spines 20' which drain 1d6 points of strength (which return 1 point/hour). In lieu of attacking, this monster can *Dispel Magic*.

2513 An otherwise-powerless 2nd-level magic-user (ARMOR: chain, HD 2, HP 9, MOVE 90') armed with long sword and dagger has a puissant familiar, a 5'-long Chinese dragon (ARMOR: as chain, HD 5, HP 23, MOVE 360', 1d8/bite) with the most ornate and intricate of golden scales, adorned with jade and azure. Five-clawed and wingless, it flies as swiftly and agilely as a hummingbird. The familiar is immune to any non-magical attack. Though it can bite, the dragon typically attacks by breathing forth shimmering colors that appear as a psychedelically vivid Aurora Borealis. All seeing it will stand hypnotically entranced (unless a saving throw is made at −2) until the lights fade after 1 turn. This breath weapon can be used once each turn. The magic-user and his familiar have unlimited telepathic contact. If the familiar is slain, the magic-user will fall to the ground stricken, reduced to 1 hit point.

2514 Atop a 15' diameter outcropping of rock 100' from shore stands a statue of a Nereid, hewn from light sea blue stone. If anyone steps upon the rocky outcropping, 9 smooth hammerhead sharks (ARMOR: as leather, HD 4, HP 23, 24, 20, 27, 20, 14, 19, 12, 29, MOVE 240', 2d4/bite) averaging 10' long will begin circling the outcropping and will attack any swimmer or small boat.

2515 The Aquatic Mage, a 4th-level magic-user (ARMOR: none, HD 4, HP 15, MOVE 360' [swim], 120' [walk]), lives amongst the seals that make their home upon this small island. Various species of aquatic mammals swim in the waters here. The Aquatic Mage can silently communicate with all of them, and they regard him as their friend. He can hold his breath for 3 turns, and he regenerates 1 HP/round when in the waters.

2616 These pine-forested islands seem unremarkable until travelers leave them. For every hour spent on the larger, western isle, one day will have passed in the rest of the world. For every hour spent on the smaller,

HEX DESCRIPTIONS

eastern isle, 15 days will have passed in the rest of the world. People leaving the islands will suffer no ill effects, other than disorientation when they discover that the date is (perhaps much) later than they thought.

MONSTERS

1 HD

0408	1203	2109
0511	1506	2203

2 HD

0806	1009	1416
1001	1111	1504

3 HD

0604	1514	2011	2310
0912	1602	2111	

4 HD

0310	1013	1305	1508
0613	1016	1309	2402
0702	1214	1404	

5 HD

0307	1406	2108	2410
0610	1503	2112	2513
0714	1613	2306	
1114	1813	2314	

117

6 HD

0312	0810	1215	1805
0711	0814	1216	2115
0803	0914	1409	

7 HD

0709	1415	1612	2412
1206	1509	2204	
1408	1608	2406	

8 HD

0407	1304	1712	2505
0905	1315	1802	
1004	1708	2213	

9 HD

0115	0708	1112	1715
0505	1014	1316	2307

10 HD

0412	1213	1611	2303
0602	1412	1711	

11 HD

1208	1906
1303	2005
1607	2212

12 HD

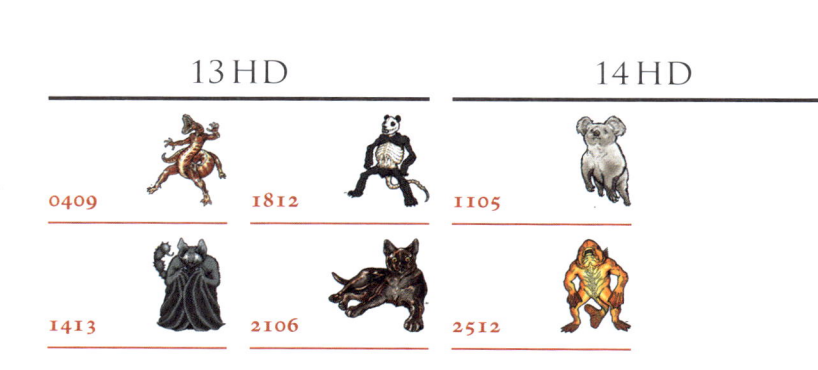

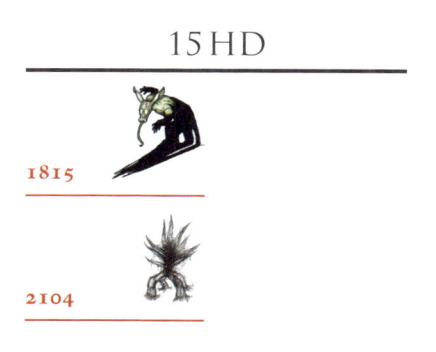

0311	1710
0608	1903
1510	

13 HD

0409	1812
1413	2106

14 HD

1105
2512

15 HD

1815
2104

120

MAGICAL STATUES

0214	iron Titan, 30' tall, holds a javelin	0816	red bearded warrior with red armor: Say please!
0314	white stone boy sprays poison	0902	nude seductress with knee-length, honey-gold hair
0315	bronze, 30' tall, wreathed in steam	0904	man with three heads (man, bull, and lion) and lower body of a snake
0405	wooden old woman grants communication with animals	0906	silver nude woman with eagle's feet and wings
0503	holds trident, in chariot pulled by seahorses	0909	white marble demure maiden that heals
0508	nude woman changes colors with the seasons	0910	man of wood-hued stone that repairs items
0514	invisible statue casts shadow	0911	golden-hued stone, nude woman who heals the lawful and good
0515	hooded man holding hourglass of time-traveling	0913	blood-red stone, smirking nude harlot, drains blood
0614	gowned woman veined with silver animated by the moon	0916	blue-green bearded man with fish tail, holds trident, stands on a river island
0705	young man carved of polished obsidian	1003	white marble, robed woman, 24' tall, holds two pan balance and sword
0716	Grecian philosopher carved of pure white ivory	1010	pure white marble, warrior with lance on a winged horse
0804	blue-gray metal, smiling man with beetles		
0805	bright yellow stone, young man with songbirds		
0811	pale green old man with horn of plagues		

1015	brownish-green rock, barbarian with eyes of wine-red garnet	1402	gold-plated, holds two silver swords, surrounded by swords
1101	pale blue crystal, long-haired woman with billowing dress, winds	1403	pale gray stone, changes form and countenance
1102	mirror-bright silver, Mercury, delivers messages	1410	iron smith, 20' tall, surrounded by illusion of gold
1103	blue-gray stone, nude woman with eagle wings, calls down lightning	1411	red-copper, long-haired nude woman holds curved knife of vengeance
1106	black Anubis in full jackal form	1515	black stone, evil-visaged man causes nightmares
1107	silver-coated man calls down lightning	1516	black stone, oozes blood, bursts into black flame
1110	translucent, icy blue stone, nude woman, points directions	1606	dark gray stone, young man with eagle's wings
1205	gray, gowned woman hiding her face, weeping before cave mouth	1702	grayish-white stone, long-haired and long-bearded elder king
1209	sky blue stone, nude woman with harp, unusual colors (illustrated on the cover)	1704	iron, naked cyclops holding a spear, flock of 99 white sheep
1210	marble beardless man, covered with dozens of eyes	1706	brown-green stone, man with hat, cloak, and walking stick, teleports
1301	colorless crystal, young man, invisibility	1709	colorless, clear crystal, glows, changes color based on alignment
1308	grim man with hammer which turns victims to stone (with 36 victims)	1714	rich purple stone, naked man emptying wine from an amphora
1311	rock covered with moss and mica, barbarian in bear's skin	1808	painted stone, scholar with bowl and vial that transmute metal of coins
1312	translucent crystal of four colors, old man, turns men into elementals	1811	bearded middle-aged man answers questions
1313	midnight blue rock, a pair standing 20' high, blindness	1902	glossy black stone, 11' tall, holds a 10' long two-handed sword
1314	sandstone, bearded man, hundreds of hawks	1907	white marble, man holds a golden ram's fleece that heals
1401	pale green limestone man, underground, desires human blood		

1908	two identical statues of matrons holding large mirrors that entrap	2214	creamy-gold stone, nude woman pours healing honey from jar
1909	gray stone, Amazon, tries to kill all males	2305	nine stone travelers in pine grove, victims of petrification
1911	rose-hued stone, nude woman with long, black hair, surrounded by eternal spring	2308	silver-plated nude woman, sings victims to sleep
1912	bronze man 10' tall, waves of pain emanate from it	2309	merry young man in checkered purple and yellow, flute induces dancing
2001	hideously-visaged statues that protect a holy shrine	2311	black-green stone Medusa, grants petrifying gaze
2007	gray stone, bearded man with hammer, enchants to remain in cave	2313	pale alabaster, nude young woman, polymorph in exchange for silver or platinum
2010	gray stone, old, bearded man in voluminous robe that affects spells	2316	jade-green stone, 25' tall crowned sea-king standing on rock at sea, causes winds
2013	two realistic women from Lesbos, surrounded by weapons	2404	gowned white woman with swan wings, gift of flight
2114	gray granite, warrior in chain with spear and short sword, benefits fighters	2407	fiery orange stone, apologetic youth missing arm burns those who touch
2202	brown-green stone, hunter with bow and arrows that polymorph into bear or mink	2413	verdigris-coated copper, impish man sticking out tongue, sprays poison
2205	alabaster, armored warrior woman holding ivory owl of wisdom	2514	light sea blue stone Nereid, atop stone in ocean surrounded by hammerhead sharks
2208	weathered white warrior, attacks those stepping on its shadow		
2210	jade, curly-haired bearded man befriended by trees		
2211	white marble, 8' tall muscular man wearing lion pelt, polymorph into *Smilodon*		

MAGIC-USERS

0215	Mage of Mirrors (6th-level)	1113	Beast Master (5th-level)
0406	clairvoyant, adolescent girl (4th-level)	1115	man with magic balance scale (9th-level)
0414	female Arabic shapechanger (5th-level)	1302	man with golden fleeced sheep (6th-level)
0509	mounted man who can speak with animals (8th-level)	1306	Loremaster (5th-level)
0606	woman with gray and green goats (7th-level)	1614	maiden with cats and butterflies (10th-level)
0611	old man, healer with snake (8th-level)	1803	woman with herd of milk-white cattle (6th-level)
0704	man with magic amphora (7th-level)	1807	Fire Wizard (5th-level)
0713	Enchantress of Petals (6th-level)	1913	man with lion-head and lions (10th-level)
0715	Chromatic Master of Hues (4th-level)	1915	seductive enchantress (4th-level)
0807	Ice Wizard (6th-level)	2006	twin young men with mercury arms and armor (11th-level)
0813	woman with eagle's wings (9th-level)	2110	woman with crabs and crab-arms (10th-level)
1002	crone who turns others into fish (7th-level)	2507	Tessellated Mage (6th-level)
1006	Alchemist (3rd-level)	2513	man with small Chinese dragon familiar (2nd-level)
		2515	Aquatic Mage (4th-level)

CLERICS

0114	bi-located across the Western Ocean (4th-level)
0308	horse-friend (4th-level)
0413	his wounds heal his friends (7th-level)
0809	never misses with a weapon (6th-level)
0815	old hermit-healer (10th-level)
1012	man with seven fair daughters (2nd-level)
1212	gardener and friend of animals (3rd-level)
1507	diabolic high priest (9th-level)
1604	summons rainbow-colored, sun-like sphere (9th-level)
2001	shrine guardian with miraculous statues (5th-level)
2107	always does maximum damage (6th-level)
2207	a solitary impervious to the elements (5th-level)
2314	cursed by being transformed into an angelfish (2nd-level)
2408	calls down torrents of fire from the heavens (7th-level)
2411	wicked impostor and corruptor (6th-level)

TOWNS

0410
0416
0506
0516
0603
0712
0812
0903
0907
1211
1809
1814
2002
2012
2103

CITY

2409

Isle of the Unknown

1 Hex = 10 Miles

- ✚ CLERIC
- ✳ MAGIC-USER
- ● MONSTER
- ◐ MAGICAL STATUE
- ◉ TOWN
- ◻ CITY